America's Most Wanted Recipes

RON DOUGLAS

The Secret Recipes for Your Favorite Dishes

Several products displayed and mentioned in this book are trademarked. The companies which own these trademarks have not participated in, nor do they endorse, this book.

This book features a compilation of recipes and cooking tips based on personal interpretation of the foods listed. Through trial and error, each recipe was recreated to taste the same as, or similar to, its restaurant/brand counterpart, but they are not the actual recipes used by the manufacturer or creator.

The brand or restaurant names for the recipes have only been included as an aid in cataloging the recipes and do not imply authenticity or endorsement by the manufacturer or creator. All restaurant and company names are trademarks of their respective owners. Please see our Trademarks section at the end of this book for detailed trademark credits.

For the actual and authentic version of the food products listed in this compilation, please patronize the individual restaurant or manufacturer.

ISBN 1-59872-395-2

To the best of the author's knowledge, all company related information and trademark details are true and accurate. Any misrepresentation of factual material is unintentional.

Printed in the United States of America
Published and distributed by Verity Associates, LLC - Kew Gardens Hills, NY

To all the friends I've made at RecipeSecrets.net over the years - thanks for inspiring me and thanks for your contributions to this cookbook.

To my daughter Nia - if this world were mine, I'd give it all to you.

To all cooking enthusiasts - You're Invited!...

Come share recipes and good times with us online at:

www.RecipeSecrets.net/forums

PREFACE

This cookbook is a compilation of 115 of the most beloved restaurant dishes in America based on our research and consumer surveys. These are the "secret recipes" which are generating billions of dollars for the restaurant industry every year. Now you can have them to prepare in your own kitchen!

Everyone enjoys eating out but there's nothing like a home cooked meal made from scratch. Why not have the best of both worlds? Enjoy these dishes made fresh at home and save money in the process.

How much can you save?
The amount you'll save depends on how many times you substitute preparing these recipes at home instead of eating out. Here's an example of the potential savings:

Fettuccini Alfredo from the Olive Garden®

Retail Price: $10.25
Home Version: $4.28
You Save: $5.97

When you consider that the home version recipe serves 6, you are actually saving $35.82. Over time, saving money this way really adds up.

How did we get these recipes?
No, we didn't sneak into the kitchens of America's favorite restaurants and run off with their secret cookbooks (although it may have been easier that way). The recipe collection in this cookbook has been researched and compiled with the help of our RecipeSecrets.net community of over 100,000 subscribers. Each recipe has been tested and tweaked to taste just like the original.

Due to intellectual property laws, we can only claim to offer "clones" of these famous dishes. However, we're confident that if you follow these instructions, you won't be able to tell the difference.

We encourage you to put the book to good use and make these famous dishes yourself. Once you've tried the recipes, you'll see what makes them so special and why we have so many satisfied customers.

You can also get thousands of additional recipes and interact with our online community through our free Secret Recipe Forum - go to: www.RecipeSecrets.net/forum.

I hope this cookbook brings enjoyment for you, your family and friends for years to come.

Ron Douglas
Author of *America's Most Wanted Recipes*

CONTENTS

Continued on next page

Recipe
Secrets
.net

Recipe
Secrets
.net

*Applebee's Baby Back Ribs

Baby back ribs basted in a sweet BBQ sauce. You'll be licking your fingers once you taste this delicious dish.. Typically served with baked beans, fries and cole slaw.

Ingredients

3 (1 lb) racks pork baby back ribs cut in half
1 cup ketchup
1/4 cup apple cider vinegar
3 tablespoon dark brown sugar
3 tablespoon Worcestershire sauce
1 teaspoon liquid smoke
1/2 teaspoon salt

1. Place ribs in a large pot and fill pot with enough water to cover ribs.
2. Bring water to a boil, reduce heat, cover and simmer for 1 hour, or until ribs are fork tender.
3. While ribs are boiling, combine remaining ingredients in a medium saucepan and bring to a boil.
4. Reduce heat and simmer, uncovered, stirring often, for 30 minutes, or until slightly thickened.
5. Place boiled ribs, meat side down, on a broiler pan.
6. Brush with half the sauce mixture and broil 4" to 5" from heat for 6-7 minutes.
7. Turn ribs over, brush with remaining sauce, and broil additional 6-7 minutes, or until edges are slightly charred.

Serves 3

RecipeSecrets.net tip: If you like your ribs falling off the bone, add 1 cup of apple cider vinegar to water before placing ribs to boil.

*Applebee's Bacon Scallion Mashed Potatoes

Applebee's® was founded in Atlanta, Georgia, by Bill and T.J. Palmer. They envisioned a restaurant that would provide full service, consistently good food, reasonable prices and quality service in a neighborhood setting. Their first restaurant, T.J. Applebee's Rx for Edibles & Elixirs®, opened in November 1980.

Ingredients

2 lbs. potatoes - peeled, cut into 1" cubes
4 cloves garlic - peeled
5 strips bacon - cut into 1/2" pieces
1 cup thinly sliced scallions
1/2 cup low fat milk - warmed
1/2 cup low fat sour cream
1 teaspoon salt
1/4 teaspoon black pepper

1. In a large pot, cover potatoes and garlic with lightly salted water.
2. Boil until potatoes are fork tender.
3. Fry bacon in skillet until crisp; drain on paper towels.
4. Pour out all but 1 teaspoon bacon grease from pan.
5. Add scallions to grease, sauté until soft, but not brown. Add bacon.
6. Drain potatoes and return to pot.
7. Mash potatoes with milk, sour cream, salt, and pepper. Stir in bacon and scallions.
8. Reheat, if necessary, before serving.

Serves 4

*Applebee's Fiesta Lime Chicken

Grilled boneless breast marinated in lime juice and tequila flavors. Typically served with crisp tortilla strips, Southwest rice and Pico de Gallo.

Ingredients

8 boned, skinned chicken breast halves
8 oz. Monterey Jack cheese - divided
1 cup Italian bread crumbs
1 1/2 tablespoon grated Parmesan cheese
1/2 teaspoon salt
1/2 teaspoon ground cumin
1/2 teaspoon black pepper
1/2 cup melted butter or margarine
1 tablespoon butter or margarine
1 tablespoon all-purpose flour
1 cup milk
1 small red bell pepper - seeded, diced
1 small green bell pepper - seeded, diced

1. Whisk together the first 8 ingredients, coat chicken in mixture, and marinade for at least 2 hours.
2. To prepare the dressing: whisk together the next 9 ingredients, cover, and chill until needed.
3. Grill the marinated chicken breasts for 3-5 minutes per side, or until cooked through. Discard marinade.
4. Brush grilled chicken with reserved dressing, sprinkle with cheese, and broil until cheese has melted.
5. Serve the chicken over a bed of crumbled chips.

Serves 4

*Applebee's Low-Fat Blackened Chicken Salad

Ingredients

2 boneless, skinless chicken breast halves
2 tablespoons butter

Dressing
1/4 cup low fat mayonnaise
1/4 cup Dijon mustard
1 tablespoon yellow mustard
1 tablespoon apple vinegar
1/4 cup honey
1/8 teaspoon paprika

Chicken Marinade
1 cup water
3 tablespoons lime juice
2 tablespoons soy sauce
1/2 tablespoon Worcestershire sauce

Cajun Spice Blend
1/2 tablespoon salt
1 teaspoon brown sugar
1 teaspoon paprika
1 teaspoon onion powder
1 teaspoon black pepper
1/2 teaspoon garlic powder
1/2 teaspoon cayenne pepper
1/2 teaspoon white pepper

Salad
8 cups chopped red leaf lettuce
1/2 cup shredded red cabbage
1/2 cup shredded carrot
1/2 cup fat free shredded mozzarella cheese
1/2 cup fat free shredded cheddar cheese
1 large tomato, diced
1 hardboiled egg white, diced

1. Mix dressing ingredients in small bowl and refrigerate until ready.
2. Mix marinade ingredients in a medium bowl. Add the chicken breasts to the marinade, cover and refrigerate overnight or at least several hours.
3. Preheat oven broiler or grill.
4. Mix Cajun spice blend ingredients in a bowl. Rub the spice into both sides of the chicken breasts until covered with spice.
5. Melt the butter in pan over medium heat. Sear chicken breasts for 2-3 minutes and flip it over so that both sides are coated with a charred black layer of spice.

6. Place chicken in broiler or on grill for an additional 2-3 minutes or until thoroughly cooked.
7. Mix ingredients for salad in a large bowl. Serve into two individual bowls.
8. Slice chicken into 1/2 inch wide slices and add to salad.
9. Serve with salad dressing on the side.

Serves 2

*Applebee's Santa Fe Chicken

Experience the flavor of the Southwest with this popular grilled marinated chicken dish. Serve over a bed of rice pilaf with mixed vegetables.

Ingredients

8 boned, skinned chicken breast halves
8 oz. block Monterey Jack cheese
- divided
1 cup Italian bread crumbs
1 1/2 Tbs. grated Parmesan cheese
1/2 teaspoon salt
1/2 teaspoon ground cumin
1/2 teaspoon black pepper
1/2 cup melted butter or margarine
1 tablespoon butter or margarine
1 tablespoon all-purpose flour
1 cup milk
1 small red bell pepper - seeded, diced
1 small green bell pepper
- seeded, diced

1. Place 1 chicken breast between two sheets of wax paper. Working from the center to the edges, pound with a meat mallet until flat and rectangular shaped. Repeat with remaining breasts.
2. Cut half of the cheese block into 8 slices; grate the remaining cheese and set aside.
3. Wrap each flattened chicken breasts around a slice of cheese; secure with wooden picks or uncooked spaghetti noodles.
4. Combine the bread crumbs, Parmesan cheese, salt, cumin, and pepper.
5. Roll the secured chicken pieces in the melted butter and then in the bread crumb mixture.
6. Place chicken breasts in a 13" x 9" x 2" baking dish, being careful not to crowd them.
7. Drizzle remaining butter over the breasts.

8. Refrigerate for 1 hour or freeze to bake later (if you decide to freeze, increase baking time by about 5-10 minutes).
9. Bake in a 400 degree F oven for 25-30 minutes, or until chicken is cooked through.
10. Melt butter in saucepan, stir in flour, whisk in milk, then bring to a simmer.
11. Stir in grated cheese, reduce heat, and simmer until thick, stirring.
12. Place chicken on plates, pour sauce over, and top with diced peppers.

Serves 8

*Applebee's Spinach Pizza

Ingredients

1/4 cup rice milk
4 tablespoons all-purpose flour
1/3 cup nutritional yeast
10 oz. pkg. frozen spinach
 - thawed, squeezed
1 medium onion - chopped
4 cloves garlic - minced
1 tablespoon olive oil
5 medium plum tomatoes
8 oz. fresh mushrooms
1 teaspoon basil
1 teaspoon parsley
1 teaspoon cayenne pepper
3 pita breads

1. Heat milk in saucepan until hot, but not boiling.
2. Stir in flour and continue stirring until sauce begins to thicken.
3. Reduce heat and add nutritional yeast and spinach.
4. Stir constantly until thick and gooey, about 3-4 min.
5. In separate pan, sauté onion and garlic in oil until onion is tender.
6. Stir in tomatoes, mushrooms, and spices. Sauté until hot throughout. Drain out any liquid.
7. Using a very sharp bread knife, split each pita bread in half to make 2 round, flat pieces.
8. Place each piece of bread on a cookie sheet or pizza pan.
9. Spread spinach sauce over each.
10. Top with tomato mixture.
11. Bake in 425 degrees F oven for 5-7 minutes. Watch closely so that the edges of the pita don't burn.

Serves 3

*Auntie Anne Pretzels

This is the recipe that built the empire! Create your own pretzels at home.

Ingredients

4 cups bread flour
1 1/2 cups 115 degrees F water
1/4 cup warm water
1 1/2 teaspoons active dry yeast
1/2 teaspoon brown sugar
1 tablespoon baking soda
pinch of salt
1 cup melted butter

1. Combine yeast, sugar, salt and 115 degrees F water into a mixing bowl and let it settle for 5-10 minutes.
2. Stir flour to mixture and knead until smooth.
3. Place dough in a lightly greased bowl, cover with a damp towel, and allow to rise at room temperature for 45 minutes.
4. Split dough into 10 equally sized pieces
5. Roll each piece into a long rope about 1/2 inch thick and shape each rope into a pretzel.
6. In a shallow dish, stir baking soda into warm water; dip pretzels into mixture; lay coated pretzel onto a lightly greased cookie sheet.
7. Bake in a 450 degrees F until golden brown (about 10 minutes).
8. Brush melted butter onto hot pretzels.

Serves 8-12

RecipeSecrets.net tip:
Dip pretzel in butter coating both sides. Add cinnamon and sugar for sweet pretzels or salt for the traditional pretzel taste.

*Benihana Hibachi Steak

Looking for a great tasting low carb dish? This Japanese steak recipe typically has less than 5g of carbs.

Ingredients

4 (5 oz.) Sirloin Steaks
4 teaspoons soybean oil
8 large mushrooms - sliced thick
1 large onion - sliced
2 cups bean sprouts
4 tablespoons soy sauce
4 dashes salt
4 dashes black pepper

1. Broil steak until rare.
2. Heat non-stick skillet and add oil to heated skillet.
3. Add onion and cook until slight brown and soft
4. Place steak cubes in skillet with mushrooms and cook to desired preparedness (i.e. rare, medium, well done).
5. Add bean sprouts and soy sauce
6. Add salt and pepper to taste.
7. Add steak sauce (typically a mustard based sauce).

Serves 4-6

*Benihana Japanese Fried Rice

Ingredients

2 1/2 cups of cooked short grain Japanese white rice
2 eggs - beaten
1 medium carrot - finely grated
1/2 cup fresh green onion - diced small
4 teaspoons soy sauce
1/2 cup peas - unfrozen
cooking oil
salt
pepper

1. Boil rice according to package instructions. Once done, empty into mixing bowl.
2. In a large skillet, heat 2 teaspoons of oil. Scramble eggs into small pieces until cooked. Empty scrambled eggs into bowl and stir together.
3. Using the same pan, add additional oil, diced onion, peas, carrot. Let simmer for 5 minutes on low heat.
4. Add several scoops of cooled rice and egg mix to skillet. Keep gradually adding a scoop at a time into the pan and mix.
6. While mixing, slowly add a little soy sauce at a time until fried rice is a golden brown color.
7. Add salt and pepper to taste.

Serves 4

*Bennigan's Onion Soup

Ingredients

1 large onion, quartered and sliced
1/4 cup butter
2 tablespoons canola oil
3 tablespoons flour
4 cups chicken broth
4 cups beef broth
8 slices from a crusty baguette
shredded Mozzarella cheese or Swiss cheese
grated Parmesan cheese

1. In a Dutch oven, slowly sauté onions in butter and oil until onions are transparent and turning yellow, but not browned. When tender, turn heat to lowest setting and add flour, stirring until well blended.
2. Add chicken and beef broths; heat through. Divide among 8 oven safe bowls.
3. Place a slice of bread on each bowl of soup. Sprinkle equal amounts of the cheeses over bread slices.
4. Place all bowls on oven rack 4 inches from heat and broil until cheese melts. Serve hot.

Serves 8

RecipeSecrets.net tip: If you're not serving 8, don't worry. Soup can be kept in the freezer for several months and still remain fresh for reheating.

*Boston Market Creamed Spinach

A unique Boston Market dish! Spinach mixed with rich cheeses, cream and garlic.

Ingredients

5 tablespoons butter or margarine - divided
1/4 cup all-purpose flour
1/4 teaspoon salt
1 cup half and half cream
4 oz. cream cheese
2 tablespoons minced onion
1 tablespoon minced garlic
2 (10 oz.) boxes frozen chopped spinach - thawed
1/4 cup water
1/4 cup grated Parmesan cheese

1. In a saucepan over medium-low heat, melt 3 tablespoons butter. Stir flour and salt into pan until creamed together.
2. Slowly stir in cream, then stir in cream cheese; increase heat to medium.
3. Constantly whisk until mixture becomes thick and smooth; remove from heat; set aside.
4. In a saucepan over medium-high heat, sauté onions and garlic in remaining butter until transparent.
5. Add spinach and water to pan; reduce heat to low; cover. Cook, stirring occasionally, for 8 minutes.
6. Stir prepared sauce and Parmesan into pan; stir until completely blended.

Serves 6

*Boston Market Dill Potato Wedges

Tender, freshly-steamed red potatoes tossed with fresh diced dill and our special garlic butter blend.

Ingredients

2 medium red potatoes - unpeeled
butter or oil spray
garlic salt
dry dill weed

1. Preheat oven to 400 degrees F.
2. Cut potatoes into lengthwise wedges and bake in oven for 45 minutes or until tender.
3. Spray the cut sides of the potatoes in cooking oil spray.
4. Dust in garlic salt and dry dill weed and pan fry until lightly brown.

Serves 2

*Boston Market Macaroni & Cheese

Ingredients

1/4 cup butter or margarine
1 tablespoon minced onion
1/4 cup all-purpose flour
2 cups milk
4 oz. processed American cheese cubed
1 teaspoon salt
1 dash black pepper
1/4 teaspoon dry mustard
1/4 lb. elbow macaroni cooked al dente (slightly chewy to the bite)

1. Sauté onions in butter until transparent.
2. Stir in flour and cook 2 minutes.
3. Slowly stir in the milk.
4. Stir in the cheese, salt, pepper, and mustard.
5. Continue to cook over medium heat, stirring constantly, until thickened.
6. Stir in prepared macaroni.
7. Lightly butter a casserole dish and pour pasta mixture to dish.
8. Bake in a 400 degrees F oven for 20 minutes.

Serves 4

*Boston Market Meatloaf

Rich, moist meatloaf is made with savory seasonings. Covered with zesty, hickory ketchup.

Ingredients

1 cup tomato sauce
1 1/2 tablespoon hickory barbecue sauce
1 tablespoon granulated sugar
1 1/2 lbs. lean ground beef
1/3 cup all-purpose flour
3/4 teaspoon salt
1/2 teaspoon onion powder
1/4 teaspoon black pepper
dash garlic powder
3/4 cup seasoned bread crumbs
1 egg

1. Stir together tomato sauce, barbecue sauce, and sugar; set aside 1/4 cup of mixture.
2. With your hands, mix in remaining ingredients.
3. Form the mixture into a loaf and place in a greased loaf pan.
4. Bake, covered, in 400 degrees F oven for 30 minutes.
5. Uncover and drain fat from the pan, then slice meatloaf while in the pan.
6. Drizzle the reserved tomato mixture evenly over the meatloaf.
7. Bake, uncovered, for an additional 30 minutes, or until cooked through.

Serves 5

*Boston Market Spicy Rice

Ingredients

1/4 cup raw rice-shaped pasta
3/4 cup minute rice
1 tablespoon pimiento - chopped fine
1/2 teaspoon dry minced celery leaf
1 teaspoon dry minced parsley
1/4 teaspoon dry mustard
14 oz can chicken broth
1/4 cup olive oil
1/2 teaspoon salt

1. In a 2-qt saucepan combine all ingredients. Stir often and bring to a boil.
2. Cover and remove from heat. Let stand 15 minutes. Fluff rice with a fork every 5 minutes.
3. Add salt and pepper to taste.

Serves 6

*Boston Market Stuffing

Ingredients

1 (14 oz.) can clear chicken broth
1 (10 oz.) can sliced carrots - undrained
1 (4 oz.) can sliced mushrooms - undrained
2 ribs celery cut in 5 pieces each
1 tablespoon rubbed sage
1/2 teaspoon poultry seasoning
1 tablespoon chicken bouillon powder
3 tablespoons bottled liquid margarine or melted butter
3 English Muffins cut into 1/2 inch cubes
1 (8 oz.) bag (6 cups) unseasoned croutons
1 tablespoon dry minced parsley
2 tablespoons dry minced onion

1. Open the can of carrots and slice them (while still in the can) with a pairing knife.
2. Empty sliced carrots into a Dutch oven. Add mushrooms; set aside.
3. Pour chicken broth into a blender. Add celery pieces, sage, poultry seasoning, bouillon powder and margarine. Blend for a few seconds or until celery is finely minced.
4. Add English muffin cubes, croutons, parsley and onion to Dutch oven.
5. Pour in blender mixture and stir with rubber bowl scraper until completely moist.
6. Cover and bake at 350° about 45 minutes or until steaming hot.

Serves 8

*Burger King Whopper

Here's the homemade version of the Whopper, without the pre-packed ingredients used at the restaurant. Of course you can also "have it your way" as the commercial says.

Ingredients

1 sesame seed hamburger bun
1/4 lb ground beef
2 dill pickle slices (flat and round)
4 sliced onion rings
2 tomato slices
chopped lettuce
mayonnaise
ketchup
dash of seasoning salt
dash of Accent flavor enhancer

1. Heat barbeque grill (medium flame).
2. Gently massage seasoning salt and Accent into ground beef.
3. Flatten hamburger meat into a flat and wide patty.
4. Cook hamburger patty on grill to desired preparedness.
5. Lightly toast both halves of the bun on grill.
6. Spread mayonnaise and ketchup on both sides of bun. Stack (in order) the bottom bun, burger, pickles, onions, tomatoes, lettuce, and top bun.

Makes 1 Whopper

*California Pizza Kitchen BBQ Chicken Pizza

The original BBQ chicken pizza introduced in the first California Pizza Kitchen restaurant in 1985 and now is their most popular pizza. A delicious and unique dish which includes BBQ Chicken, barbecue sauce, smoked Gouda and Mozzarella cheeses.

Ingredients

cornmeal, semolina, or flour for handling
1/2 cup Bullseye Original barbecue sauce
2 tablespoons shredded smoked Gouda cheese
1 cup shredded mozzarella cheese
commercial pizza dough or dough mix
1/2 small red onion, sliced into 1/2 inch pieces
2 tablespoons chopped fresh cilantro
1 boneless, skinless chicken breast half
1 tablespoon olive oil

1. Cook chicken in large frying pan over medium heat for 5-6 minutes. Be careful not to over cook. Set aside in refrigerator.
2. Once chicken is chilled, coat with barbeque sauce and set aside.
3. Follow instructions on the commercial pizza dough or dough mix to prepare enough dough for a 10-inch crust. Form pizza dough into a ball and roll out over a floured surface until 10 inches wide, round and flat.
4. Put pizza crust onto a baking sheet and spread remaining barbeque sauce evenly over crust.

5. Sprinkle 1/2 cup of mozzarella and the gouda cheese over sauce.
6. Add barbeque chicken, red onion, and cover with remaining 1/2 cup of mozzarella. Add cilantro on top of the mozzarella.
7. Bake for 10 minutes or until crust is crisp and golden.

Serves 6-8

*Chi Chi's Baked Chicken Chimichangas

Since 1976, Chi Chi's restaurants have been known for their fun atmosphere and great Mexican style food. Today you can get many of their great products in your local supermarket.

Ingredients

1 pound boneless, skinless chicken, cooked and shredded
2 tablespoons olive oil
1/2 cup chopped onion
2 cloves garlic, minced
1/3 cup chili powder
1 Chi-Chi's® Salsa (16-oz.) jar
4 tablespoons water
1/2 teaspoon ground cumin
1/2 teaspoon cinnamon
Salt
6 (10-inch) flour tortillas, warmed
1 cup Chi-Chi's® Refried Beans
olive oil
sour cream
guacamole

1. In large saucepan, sauté onion and garlic in oil until tender. Stir in chili powder, salsa, water, cumin and cinnamon. Pour mixture into blender container or food processor bowl fitted with metal blade. Process until smooth. Pour back into saucepan; stir in chicken. Add salt to taste.
2. Heat oven to 425 degrees F. Grease rimmed 15"x10"x1"-inch baking pan. Working with 1 tortilla at a time (keep remaining tortillas wrapped), spoon a heaping tablespoon of beans down center of each tortilla. Top with about 1/2 cup chicken mixture. Fold up the bottom, top and sides of tortilla; secure with wooden picks, if necessary.
3. Place chimichangas in greased baking pan, seam-side-down. Brush all sides with oil.
4. Bake 15 minutes or until golden brown and crisp, turning every 5 minutes. Serve with salsa, sour cream and guacamole.

Serves 6

*Chi Chi's Pork Tenderloin with Bourbon Sauce

Ingredients

10 oz can Chi Chi's diced tomatoes and green chilies, drained
1/3 cup Bourbon
1/3 cup Soy sauce
1/3 cup Worcestershire sauce
1/2 cup Chopped onion
2 tablespoons Honey
2 tablespoons Dijon mustard
1/4 teaspoon Pepper
2 pounds Pork tenderloin

1. Combine all marinade ingredients in reclosable plastic food bag. Mix well. Add the pork tenderloin. Seal bag and turn several times to coat the meat. Place in refrigerator for 8 hours or overnight, turning occasionally.
2. Preheat broiler. Remove meat from marinade; reserve marinade.
3. Place meat on broiler pan, broil 7 to 8 inches from heat source for approximately 7 to 9 minutes on each side.
4. In small saucepan, bring remainder of marinade to a boil; boil one minute. Serve with the meat.

Serves 4

*Chi Chi's Salsa Verde Chicken Kabobs

If you're looking for a great tasting break from the norm, this dish is for you. I tried it with Plantains instead of bananas and it came out great.

Ingredients

16 oz. Chi-Chi Salsa Verde
(available at grocery stores)
1/4 cup olive oil
2 tablespoons lime juice
3 cloves garlic
1 boneless skinless chicken breast cut into 1 1/2 inch strips
2 cups finely shredded cabbage
1 1/2 cup finely juilienned jicama
1 cup shredded carrot
1/3 cup coarsely chopped fresh cilantro
1 dash salt to taste
1 dash pepper to taste
2 large ripe bananas

* *If Chi-Chi's Salsa Verde is not available in your area, look for a salsa made from tomatillos, fresh cilantro and fresh onions. Spicy and sweet!*

1. In blender container or food processor combine salsa verde, oil, lime and garlic. Process until smooth.
2. Remove 2/3 cup of this mix and set aside. Refrigerate.
3. Place chicken in re-closeable plastic food storage bag; pour the remaining salsa mixture over the chicken. Seal bag and turn over several times to coat pieces thoroughly. Refrigerate, turning bag occasionally for at least four hours or overnight.
4. In large bowl, combine vegetables and cilantro. Stir in the reserved 2/3 cup salsa verde mixture. Add salt and pepper to taste - set aside.

5. Thread chicken pieces onto 8 long bamboo skewers (be sure to presoak the skewers in water 30 mins. before using). Cook over medium hot coals, grill kabobs five minutes on each side or until no longer pink in the center.
6. Slice bananas lengthwise, grill two minutes on each side.
7. Serve chicken and bananas on top of cabbage mixture.

Serves 2

*Chi Chi's Steak and Mushroom Quesadillas

Ingredients

4 oz. flap or skirt steak marinated in soy sauce, pineapple juice, garlic, salt and black pepper
1 oz. sliced red peppers
1 oz. sliced green peppers
1 oz. sliced yellow onions
2 oz. sliced mushrooms
1 oz. garlic butter
1 (12") Jalapeno Cheddar or Flour Tortilla
3 oz. Monterey Jack and Cheddar Cheese Blend
3 oz. Fresh Pico de Gallo
1 oz. Shredded Iceberg Lettuce
1 oz. Guacamole
1 oz. Sour Cream
2 oz. Chi-Chi's Brand Chile con Queso or other dipping sauce

For Pico De Gallo:
1 pound Diced Roma Tomatoes
3 oz. Diced Yellow Onions
1/2 oz. Chopped Fresh Cilantro
Salt, pepper, granulated garlic and fresh lime juice to taste

1. Marinate the steak for at least 2 hours prior to grilling. Grill steak to preferred doneness. Remove the steak from the grill and slice thinly.
2. Sauté the red peppers, green peppers, yellow onions and mushrooms in the garlic butter until the vegetables are semi-soft and have a light golden color to them.
3. Lay the tortilla on a medium heat grill or large sauté pan. Top the tortilla with the cheese, Pico de Gallo, sautéed vegetables and the grilled steak.
4. Allow to heat until the cheese has melted. Once the cheese has melted, fold the tortilla in half. Remove the tortilla from the heat and cut into four wedges.
5. Place the cut tortilla on a large serving plate and finish off with shredded lettuce, sour cream, guacamole and Chile con Queso for dipping.

Serves 4

*Chili's Baby Back Ribs

I want my "baby-back baby-back baby-back ribs." This is the dish that Chili's is famous for. Full rack of ribs "double-basted" w/BBQ sauce. Typically served w/cinnamon apples & homestyle fries.

Ingredients

6 pounds baby back pork ribs
2 cups water

Sauce

1 cup white vinegar
1/2 cup tomato paste
1 tablespoon yellow mustard
1/4 cup dark brown sugar
1 teaspoon liquid hickory flavoring
3 tablespoons Worcestershire sauce
1 1/4 teaspoons salt
1/2 teaspoon onion powder
1/4 teaspoon garlic powder
1/4 teaspoon paprika

1. Preheat oven to 350 degrees F.
2. Cut the rib slabs in half, leaving 6 to 8 ribs per section. In a large roasting pan, arrange the ribs evenly, then add the water. Cover pan tightly with a lid or foil to prevent steam from escaping. Bake for 3 hours.
3. About 2 hours into the baking time, make the sauce. In a large saucepan, combine all the sauce ingredients. Simmer over low heat for 1 hour, stirring occasionally.
4. Prepare the coals in a barbecue. Remove the ribs from the roasting pan. Discard the water.

5. Cover the ribs with sauce, saving about 1-1/2 cups of the sauce for later use at the table. Grill the ribs on the barbecue for about 5 minutes per side, or until slightly charred.
6. Serve with the remaining sauce and lots of moist towelettes or paper towels.

Serves 6-8

Chili's Boneless Buffalo Wings

Breaded chicken breast tossed in spicy wing sauce. Served with cool bleu cheese dressing.

Ingredients

1 cup flour
2 tablespoons salt
1/2 teaspoon black pepper
1/4 teaspoon cayenne
1/4 teaspoon paprika
1 egg
1 cup milk
1/2 cup buffalo wing hot sauce
2 chicken breasts, sliced into multiple 2 inch squares

1. Mix flour, salt, pepper and paprika in a bowl.
2. In another bowl mix egg and milk.
3. Heat deep fryer or wok with oil.
4. Dip chicken pieces in egg mixture then cover with flour mixture. Repeat again and then add to hot oil to fry.
5. When the chicken is done, drain grease on paper towels.
6. Arrange the pieces in a container and drizzle with hot sauce mixture. Gently shake to cover chicken pieces in sauce.
7. Serve immediately with celery stalks and blue-cheese dip.

Serves 2-4

*Chili's Chicken Enchilada Soup

Ingredients

1/2 cup vegetable oil
1/4 cup chicken base
3 cups diced yellow onions
2 teaspoons ground cumin
2 teaspoons chili powder
2 teaspoons granulated garlic
1/2 teaspoon cayenne pepper
2 cups masa harina
4 qts. water, divided
2 cups crushed tomatoes
1/2 lb. Velveeta cheese, cubed
3 lbs. boneless, chicken breasts, cooked and shredded

Garnish

cheddar cheese
tortilla chips
Pico de Gallo

1. In large pot, place oil, chicken base, onion and spices. Sauté until onions are soft and clear, about 5 minutes.
2. In another container, combine masa harina with 1 quart water. Stir until all lumps dissolve. Add to sautéed onions and bring to boil. Cook an additional 2-3 minutes, stirring constantly.
3. Add remaining water to pot. Add tomatoes and return to a boil, stirring occasionally. Add cheese and stir until it melts. Add chicken; heat and serve.
4. Garnish with shredded cheddar cheese, crumbled tortilla chips, and Pico de Gallo.

Serves 16-20

*Chili's Fajitas

Juicy, marinated chicken or steak grilled to perfection! Served sizzling with onions and bell peppers.

Ingredients

1/4 cup lime juice
2 tablespoons olive oil
4 cloves garlic - crushed
2 teaspoons soy sauce
1 teaspoon salt
1/2 teaspoon liquid smoke
1/2 teaspoon cayenne pepper
1/4 teaspoon black pepper
1 lb. boned, skinned chicken breasts or sirloin steak
2 tablespoons water
1 teaspoon soy sauce
1/2 teaspoon lime juice
1 dash salt
1 dash black pepper
1 tablespoon olive oil
1 large Spanish onion - sliced thin
1/2 medium green bell pepper - seeded, sliced thin
1/2 medium red bell pepper - seeded, sliced thin

1. Combine 1/4 cup lime juice, 2 tablespoons oil, garlic, 2 teaspoons soy sauce, 1 teaspoon salt, liquid smoke, cayenne pepper, 1/4 teaspoon black pepper, and either the sirloin or the chicken in a sealable plastic container, cover and refrigerate for at least 2 hours, or overnight.
2. Combine water, 1 teaspoon soy sauce, 1/2 teaspoon lime juice, salt, and 1 dash black pepper; set aside.
3. Grill meat over a medium high flame 4 to 5 minutes on each side.
4. Cut meat into thin strips; set aside and keep warm.
5. Cook onion and bell peppers in oil until brown; remove from heat.
6. Pour reserved liquid mixture over onions and bell peppers.
7. Combine meat, onions, and bell peppers.

Serves 4

*Chili's Southwest Chicken Chili

Ingredients

1/4 cup vegetable oil
1/2 cup diced onions
1 1/3 cup diced green bell pepper
2 tablespoons diced seeded jalapenos pepper
3 tablespoons fresh minced garlic
4 1/2 cups water
8 teaspoons chicken base
2 teaspoons lime juice
2 tablespoons sugar
3 tablespoons cornstarch
3 tablespoons ground cumin
2 1/2 tablespoons ground chili powder
4 teaspoons ground paprika
4 teaspoons dried basil
2 teaspoons freshly-minced cilantro
1 1/2 teaspoon ground red pepper
1/2 teaspoon ground oregano
1/2 cup crushed canned tomatillos
1 can diced green chiles - (4 oz) - drained
2 cans navy or small white beans - (15 oz ea) - drained
1 can dark red kidney beans - (15 oz) - drained
3 pounds diced cooked chicken breast

Garnish
shredded cheese
sour cream
tortilla chips

1. In 5-quart or larger pot, heat oil over medium heat. Add onions and sauté along with bell pepper, jalapenos and garlic. Cook until vegetables are tender.
2. In another container, combine water, chicken base, lime juice, sugar, cornstarch and seasonings. Add to vegetable mixture.
3. Add tomatillos and diced green chiles to pot; bring to boil. Add beans and chicken; simmer 10 minutes.
4. Serve topped with shredded cheese and sour cream if desired, with tortilla chips on the side.

Serves 4

*Chili's Southwestern Egg Rolls

Crispy flour tortillas wrapped around smoked chicken, black beans, corn, and jalapenos Jack cheese w/red peppers and spinach. Served with a creamy avocado-ranch dipping sauce.

Ingredients

- 2 tablespoons vegetable oil
- 1 skinless, boneless chicken breast half
- 2 tablespoons minced green onion
- 2 tablespoons minced red bell pepper
- 1/3 cup frozen corn kernels
- 1/4 cup black beans, rinsed and drained
- 2 tablespoons diced jalapeno peppers
- 1/2 tablespoon minced fresh parsley
- 1/2 teaspoon ground cumin
- 1/2 teaspoon chili powder
- 1/3 teaspoon salt
- 1 pinch ground cayenne pepper
- 2 tablespoons frozen chopped spinach, thawed and drained
- 3/4 cup shredded Monterey Jack cheese
- 5 (6 inch) flour tortillas
- 1 quart oil for deep frying

1. Rub 1 tablespoon vegetable oil over chicken breast. In a medium saucepan over medium heat, cook chicken approximately 5 minutes per side, until meat is no longer pink and juices run clear. Remove from heat and set aside.
2. Heat remaining 1 tablespoon vegetable oil in a medium saucepan over medium heat. Stir in green onion and red pepper. Cook and stir 5 minutes, until tender.
3. Dice chicken and mix into the pan with onion and red pepper. Mix in corn, black beans, spinach, jalapeno peppers, parsley, cumin, chili powder, salt and cayenne pepper. Cook and stir 5 minutes, until well blended and tender. Remove from heat and stir in Monterey Jack cheese so that it melts.
4. Wrap tortillas with a clean, lightly moist cloth. Microwave on high approximately 1 minute.

5. Spoon even amounts of the mixture into each tortilla. Fold ends of tortillas, then roll tightly around mixture. Secure with toothpicks. Arrange in a medium dish, cover with plastic, and place in the freezer. Freeze at least 4 hours.
6. In a large, deep skillet, heat oil for deep frying to 375 degrees F (190 degrees C). Deep fry frozen, stuffed tortillas 10 minutes each, or until dark golden brown. Drain on paper towels before serving.
7. Slice each egg roll diagonally lengthwise and arrange on a plate around a small bowl of the dipping sauce. Garnish the dipping sauce with the chopped tomato and onion.

Serves 5-6

*Chili's Southwestern Vegetable Soup

Ingredients

6 cups chicken broth
1 (14.5-oz.) can diced tomatoes, with juice
1 cup water
1 cup canned dark red kidney beans, with liquid
1 cup frozen yellow cut corn
1 cup frozen cut green beans
1 small diced green pepper
1/2 cup diced Spanish onion
1/2 cup tomato sauce
6 corn tortillas, minced
1 1/2 teaspoons chili powder
dash garlic powder

Garnish
1 cup grated cheddar
1 cup crumbled corn tortilla chips

1. Mix soup ingredients in pot over high heat.
2. Bring soup to a boil, reduce heat and let simmer for 45 minutes.
3. Serve in a soup bowl and garnish with cheese and then add the crumbled tortilla chips on top of the cheese.

Serves 5

*Cinnabon Cinnamon Buns

Warm dough, filled with cinnamon, topped with freshly made sweet glaze frosting. A delicious and irresistible treat.

Ingredients

- 1 cup 110 degrees F water
- 2 (.25 oz.) pkts.- active dry yeast
- 2 1/2 cups + 1 teaspoon granulated sugar - divided
- 1 cup warm milk
- 2 1/3 cup melted margarine - divided
- 2 teaspoons salt
- 2 eggs - slightly beaten
- 8 cups all-purpose flour
- 3 tablespoons ground cinnamon
- 1 1/2 cups chopped walnuts or pecans
- 4 cups powdered sugar
- 2 teaspoons vanilla extract
- 1 teaspoon maple extract
- 6 tablespoons hot water

1. Dissolve yeast and 1 teaspoon sugar in warm water; set aside.
2. In a large bowl, mix 2/3 cup sugar, milk, 2/3 cup margarine, salt, and eggs; stir and add to yeast mixture.
3. Add half the flour and beat until smooth.
4. Stir in enough of the remaining flour until dough is slightly stiff.
5. Turn out onto a well-floured board and knead for 8 minutes.
6. Place dough in a greased bowl, cover, and let rise in a warm place until doubled in size, 1 - 1 1/2 hours.
7. Punch down dough and let rest for 5 minutes.

8. Roll dough out on floured surface into a 15" X 20" rectangle.
9. Brush 1/2 cup melted margarine over dough.
10. Mix together 1 1/2 cups sugar and cinnamon; sprinkle over dough.
11. Sprinkle with nuts, if desired.
12. Roll up dough and pinch edge together to seal.
13. Cut the roll into 12-15 slices.
14. Coat bottom of a 13" X 9" X 2" baking pan with 1/2 cup melted margarine, then sprinkle with 1/3 cup sugar.
15. Place cinnamon roll slices close together in pan - cover pan and allow to rise in a warm place for 45 minutes.
16. Bake in a 350 degrees F oven for 25-30 minutes, or until golden brown.
17. Stir together 2/3 cup melted margarine, powdered sugar, and extracts.
18. Stir in hot water, 1 tablespoon at a time, until glaze reaches desired spreading consistency.
19. Spread prepared icing over slightly cooled rolls.

Serves 12-15

*Dairy Queen Heath Blizzard

Ingredients

2 Heath candy bars - frozen
1/2 cup milk
4 cups vanilla ice cream
2 teaspoon fudge topping

RecipeSecrets.net tip:
You can also make this delicious dessert with: Butterfinger candy bars, Oreo cookies, and Reeses Peanut Butter Cups. For a reduced fat treat use vanilla frozen yogurt and low fat milk.

1. Bash candy into small pieces before removing it from wrapper.
2. Add all ingredients to a blender and blend until it's mixed nice and creamy.
3. To increase thickness, place in the freezer for 20 to 30 minutes.

Makes 2-3 servings

*El Pollo Loco Chicken

El Pollo Loco, pronounced "L-Po-yo Lo-co" is Spanish for "The Crazy Chicken." This restaurant started out in 1975 as a roadside chicken stand in Mexico. It's success spread rapidly throughout Mexico and into the US. Billed as "a wholesome, delicious alternative to traditional fast food faire."

Ingredients

1 whole frying chicken - quartered
2 cups water
1 teaspoon lime juice
2 tablespoons pineapple juice
1 garlic clove
4 teaspoons salt
2 teaspoons pepper
1 pinch of ground saffron

1. Combine water, garlic, salt, pepper, and saffron in a blender and blend on high speed for 15-20 seconds. Add lime juice and pineapple juice to the mix and blend for an additional 5 seconds.
2. Place mixture in a bowl. Add in chicken and let it marinate for one hour.
3. Preheat grill to a low flame.
4. Cook chicken on the grill over a low flame for about 45 minutes or until the skin is golden and crispy. Turn the chicken frequently as it cooks and try not to let the flames blacken the chicken before the center is cooked.

Serves 4-6

*El Pollo Loco (Pollo Asada)

Ingredients

1 whole chicken
1 cup white wine vinegar
1 cup olive oil
1/2 cup white wine
dash of oregano
dash of thyme
dash of salt
10 milliliters garlic - minced
1 1/2 teaspoons hot sauce

1. Mix all ingredients in a bowl.
2. Add chicken to the bowl, cover.
3. Marinate several hours in refrigerator - overnight works best.
4. Grill chickens slowly until done.
5. Serve with Mexican rice and beans or in a soft tortilla.

Serves 4

*General Tso's Chicken

General Tso's chicken is a sweet and spicy deep-fried Hunan Chinese dish that is popularly served in American and Canadian Chinese restaurants.

Ingredients

1 lb chicken thighs, boned and cubed
3 eggs - beaten
1/2 cup and 2 teaspoons cornstarch
5 dried pepper pods
1 1/2 tablespoons rice vinegar
2 tablespoons rice wine
3 tablespoons sugar
3 tablespoons soy sauce

RecipeSecrets.net tip: The traditional sauce for General Tso's is a heavy, spicy glaze, different from the lighter broth-based sauces found on most other Chinese dishes. Some prefer a lighter sauce, which can be achieved by tripling the cornstarch in the sauce and adding a half-cup chicken broth, water, or fruit. Cook the sauce only until it thickens, instead of waiting for a glaze.

1. In a large bowl, thoroughly blend the 1/2 cup of cornstarch and the eggs; add the chicken and toss to coat. If the mixture bonds too well, add some vegetable oil to separate the pieces.
2. In a small bowl, prepare the sauce mixture by combining the 2 table-spoons cornstarch with the wine, vinegar, sugar and soy sauce.
3. Heat 1-2 inches of peanut oil in a wok to medium-high heat (350-400 degrees F). Fry the chicken in small batches, just long enough to cook the chicken through. Remove the chicken to absorbent paper and allow to stand.

4. Leave a tablespoon or two of the oil in the wok. Add the pepper pods to the oil and stir-fry briefly, awakening the aroma but not burning them. Return the chicken to the wok and stir-fry until the pieces are crispy brown.
5. The General's Secret Sauce: Add the sauce-mixture to the wok, tossing over the heat until the sauce caramelizes into a glaze (1-2 minutes).
6. Serve with steamed broccoli and rice.

Serves 4

*Hard Rock Cafe BBQ Beans

Hard Rock Café was started in 1971 in London as a "specialty theme" restaurant catering to Rock & Roll lovers worldwide. They have become the world's leading collector and exhibitor of Rock & Roll memorabilia which can be seen on display in their restaurants.
All this and great food as well.

Ingredients

2 (15-oz) cans pinto beans (with liquid)
2 tablespoons water
2 teaspoons cornstarch
1/2 cup ketchup
1/3 cup white vinegar
1/4 cup brown sugar
2 tablespoons diced onion
1 teaspoon prepared mustard
1/2 teaspoon chili powder
1/4 teaspoon salt
1/4 teaspoon coarse ground black pepper
1/2 cup cooked bacon

1. Preheat oven to 350 degrees F.
2. Pour entire contents of the can of pinto beans into a casserole dish.
3. Dissolve the cornstarch in a small bowl with the 2 tablespoons of water. Add this solution to the beans and stir.
4. Add the remaining ingredients to the dish, stir well and cover.
5. Bake for 90 minutes or until the sauce thickens. Stir every 30 minutes. After removing the beans from the oven, let the beans cool for 5 to 10 minutes before serving.

Serves 6

*Hard Rock Cafe BBQ Ribs

Ingredients

3-1/2 slab St. Louis ribs, thawed
2 cups water
2 cups liquid smoke flavoring

Sauce:
1/4 cup chicken stock
2 cups ketchup
1 tsp. maple syrup
1/3 tsp. garlic powder
1/4 tsp. black pepper
2-1/2 Tbs. salad oil
1-3/4 tsp. liquid smoke
1 tsp. yellow mustard
1-1/4 Tbs. brown sugar
1-1/2 Tbs. Worcestershire sauce
1 bay leaf
3 Tbs. white vinegar
3 Tbs. orange juice

1. In a large container, mix water and liquid smoke.
2. Place thawed rib racks into this marinade for 15 minutes.
3. Place ribs in roasting pan and cover with aluminum foil. Bake at 375 degrees in a convection oven for 2 hours or in a conventional oven for 3 hours, or until fully cooked and just tender. Remove from oven and allow ribs to cool at room temperature -- no more than 30 minutes. At this point you can cover, label, date and place in the refrigerator for cooking later.
4. For the barbecue sauce, place chicken stock, ketchup, maple syrup, garlic powder, black pepper, salad oil, liquid smoke, yellow mustard, brown sugar, Worcestershire sauce and bay leaf in a large stockpot and bring to a boil.
5. Add white vinegar and orange juice and simmer for another 5 minutes. Don't over boil because the orange juice and vinegar will make the sauce bitter. Remove and discard the bay leaf after the cooking process.
6. Place cooked ribs on the grill, bone side down, and then turn them over to grill the meat. Turn bone side up and brush with the barbecue sauce. When hot, remove from the grill. Brush with additional sauce before serving.

Serves 6

*Hard Rock Cafe Homemade Chicken Noodle Soup

This traditional chicken noodle soup is a classic American dish. Cut the chicken pieces to your desired thickness to make it more or less "chunky." Serve with soup crackers.

Ingredients

- 1 pound chicken breast fillets
- 1 pound chicken thigh fillets
- vegetable oil
- 2 tablespoons butter
- 1 cup chopped onion
- 1/2 cup diced celery
- 4 cups chicken stock
- 2 cups water
- 1 cup sliced carrot
- 1 teaspoon salt
- 1/2 teaspoon pepper
- 1/2 teaspoon minced fresh parsley
- 2 cups egg noodles
- minced fresh parsley for garnish
- 2 cups of soup crackers

1. Preheat oven to 350 degrees F.
2. Grease a baking sheet with vegetable oil. Add chicken and bake for 30 minutes. Remove from oven - set aside.
3. In a large saucepan, melt the butter over medium heat. Add the onion and celery and lightly sauté for 4 minutes.
4. Dice chicken into small pieces and add it to the pot along with the remaining ingredients, except the noodles.
5. Bring the soup to a boil, reduce the heat and simmer for 30 minutes.
6. Add the noodles and simmer for an additional 15 minutes, or until the noodles are tender. Serve with a pinch of minced fresh parsley sprinkled on top and with soup crackers.

Serves 6

*Hard Rock Cafe Potato Soup

Ingredients

8 slices bacon
1 cup diced yellow onions
2/3 cup flour
6 cups hot chicken stock
4 cups diced baked potato - peeled
2 cups heavy cream
1/4 cup chopped parsley
1 1/2 teaspoon granulated garlic
1 1/2 teaspoon dried basil
1 1/2 teaspoon salt
1 1/2 teaspoon red pepper sauce
1 1/2 teaspoon coarse black pepper
1 cup grated cheddar cheese
1/4 cup diced green onions

Garnish
grated cheese
chopped parsley
bacon bits

1. Fry bacon until crisp. Chop bacon and reserve drippings. Cook onions in remaining drippings over medium-high heat until transparent, about 3 minutes.
2. Add in flour. Stir frequently to prevent lumps. Cook for 3 - 5 minutes or until mix becomes golden.
3. Gradually add in chicken stock and let cook until liquid thickens.
4. Reduce heat to simmer and add potatoes, cream, chopped bacon, parsley, garlic, basil, salt, pepper sauce and black pepper. Let simmer for 8-10 minutes.
5. Add in grated cheese and green onions and simmer until cheese melts smoothly. Garnish each serving as desired with bacon bits, grated cheese and chopped parsley.

Serves 8

*Hard Rock Cafe Shrimp Fajitas

Ingredients

1 pound medium shrimp, shelled
1 cup chopped cilantro
2 cloves minced garlic
1/3 cup lime juice
4 (9-inch) flour tortillas
1 tablespoon olive oil
2 large bell peppers, thinly sliced
1 large onion, thinly sliced
1/2 cup sour cream

1. Stir together shrimp, cilantro, garlic, and lime juice. Let stand at room temperature for 20 minutes.
2. Meanwhile, wrap tortillas in foil and place in a 350 degrees F oven until hot (about 15 minutes).
3. Heat oil in a wide nonstick frying pan over medium-high heat. Add peppers and onion. Cook, stirring occasionally, until limp (about 10 minutes). Remove vegetables and keep warm.
4. Add shrimp mixture to pan, increase heat to high, and cook, stirring often, until shrimp are opaque in center; cut to test (about 3 minutes). Return vegetables to pan, stirring to mix with shrimp.
5. Spoon shrimp mixture into tortillas, top with sour cream, and roll up.

Serves 4

*Hooter's Buffalo Wings

Everyone loves Hooter's nearly world famous chicken wings!

Ingredients

vegetable oil (for frying)
4 tablespoons butter
1/4 cup Crystal Louisiana Hot Sauce
dash of ground pepper
dash of garlic powder
1/2 cup all-purpose flour
1/4 teaspoon paprika
1/4 teaspoon cayenne pepper
1/4 teaspoon salt
10 chicken wings - cut into thirds (wing tips discarded)
bleu cheese dressing
celery sticks

1. Pour 2 inches of oil into deep fryer and heat to 375 degrees F.
2. In small saucepan, melt butter over low heat. Add hot sauce, black pepper and garlic powder and stir until well mixed.
3. In a gallon size zip-lock bag, mix flour, paprika, cayenne pepper and salt .
4. Rinse chicken wings under cold water and drain excess water. Drop wings into bag a few at a time, shaking to coat after each addition. When all wings have been coated, remove from bag and place on wax paper-lined plate or tray. Refrigerate at least 1 hour to help set coating.
5. Preheat oven to 400 degrees F.
6. Carefully lower a few wings at a time into oil. Fry 15-20 minutes or till light brown. Drain wings on paper towel and repeat with remaining wings.

7. Place cooked wings in large oven-proof bowl or baking pan; pour sauce over wings and stir to coat thoroughly.
8. Place in oven 5 minutes or so to make sure all wings are served hot.
9. Serve wings with celery sticks and bleu cheese dressing on the side.

Serves 2-3 as an appetizer

*Houston's Buttermilk Garlic Dressing

Ingredients

2/3 cup sour cream
1 cup mayonnaise
1/4 teaspoon crushed garlic
1/2 teaspoon salt
1 teaspoon paprika
1/2 teaspoon freshly ground pepper
1 teaspoon mustard powder
2 Tablespoons sugar
1/2 cup buttermilk

1. Blend all in blender until smooth.
2. Let it set for a couple hours.

Serves 4

*Houston's Spinach and Artichoke Dip

I've never liked spinach but after trying this recipe at a Houston's restaurant in midtown New York City, I was hooked. I made this dish for my wife's birthday party and many of the guests said it was the best spinach dip they've ever tasted!

Ingredients

(2) 10 oz. boxes frozen spinach - thawed
1/4 cup real butter
1 tablespoon minced fresh garlic
2 tablespoon minced onion
1/4 cup all-purpose flour
1 pint heavy cream
1/4 cup chicken stock
2 teaspoon fresh lemon juice
1/2 teaspoon hot sauce
1/2 teaspoon salt
2/3 cup grated fresh Pecorino Romano cheese
1/4 cup sour cream
1/2 cup shredded white cheddar
12 oz. jar artichoke hearts - drained, coarsely chopped

1. Strain spinach and squeeze through a cheesecloth to remove as much liquid as possible; mince; set aside.
2. In heavy saucepan over medium heat, sauté garlic and onions in butter until golden, about 3 to 5 minutes.
3. Stir in flour and cook for 1 minute.
4. Slowly whisk in cream and stock and cook until boiling.
5. Once boiling, stir in lemon juice, hot sauce, salt, and Romano cheese; stir until cheese has melted.
6. Remove from heat and allow to cool for 5 minutes.
7. Stir in sour cream, then fold in dry spinach and artichoke hearts.
8. Sprinkle cheddar evenly over top.
9. Microwave to melt cheese and serve.

Serves 12

*IHOP Colorado Omelet

A meat lover's delight. Bacon, sausage, shredded beef, ham, onions, green peppers and Cheddar cheese. Serve with salsa.

Ingredients

1/4 cup diced sweet onions
1/4 cup diced bell pepper
1/4 cup diced tomatoes
1/4 cup diced cooked lean ham
3/4 cup finely shredded cheddar cheese (reserve 1/4 cup for garnish)
1/4 cup diced lean fried bacon
1/3 cup sliced small breakfast sausage links (browned)
1/3 cup shredded roast beef or dice roasted beef from the deli
3 - 4 eggs - beaten
1/8 cup water
1/4 teaspoon salt
1 tablespoon butter

1. In a sauce pan on medium low heat melt butter and add onions and bell peppers.
2. Stir until onions and pepper are soft but not browned.
3. Add diced ham and stir until the ham is limp and heated through.
4. Immediately remove from heat and set a side.
5. In a mixing bowl add eggs, water and salt beat and stir well. Set aside.
6. Heat a 12" non stick frying pan on medium low heat, add a little oil (1 teaspoon) or spray with a non stick vegetable spray.

RecipeSecrets.net tip: For a healthier dish, you can substitute eggs with egg whites or your favorite egg substitute and use turkey meat.

7. Place egg mixture in pan and sprinkle with onions, bell pepper, ham, tomato if you wish, sausage, bacon, and 1/2 of the roast beef, and 1/2 cup of the shredded cheese.
8. Place a lid on until omelet starts to set.
9. Immediately remove lid and fold omelet from the sides to the middle or fold in half. Sprinkle with the rest of cheese and roast beef.

Serves 2

*IHOP Cream Of Wheat Pancakes

Ingredients

3-1/2 cups plain non fat yogurt
4 tablespoons honey
1 pound 11 ounces pancake mix (complete)
1 pound 2 ounces Cream of Wheat cereal, uncooked
2 teaspoons baking powder
5-1/2 cups skim milk
8 eggs, beaten
1 cup vegetable oil

1. Mix yogurt and honey until smooth, cover and reserve in refrigerator.
2. Combine pancake mix, cereal, and baking powder, reserve.
3. In a large bowl, combine milk, eggs, and vegetable oil; stir in dry ingredients.
4. For each serving ladle 3 scant 2 ounce portions of batter onto a medium-hot lightly greased griddle. Cook until pancake tops begin to bubble, flip. Cook until golden.
5. Serve with 2 ounces of the yogurt and honey mixture. Garnish with fresh fruit.

Serves 12

*IHOP Pancakes

Ingredients

1 1/4 cups all-purpose flour, stirred or sifted before measuring
1 teaspoon baking powder
1 teaspoon baking soda
pinch of salt
1 egg - slightly beaten
1 1/4 cups buttermilk
2 tablespoons melted butter
1/4 cup granulated sugar

1. Sift together flour, baking powder, baking soda, and salt.
2. In a separate bowl, combine egg and buttermilk. Add to flour mixture, stirring only until smooth.
3. Blend in melted butter and sugar.
4. Cook on a pre-heated, greased griddle, using about 1/4 cup of batter for each pancake. Drop batter on griddle in 5 inch wide segments.
5. Cook until brown on one side and around edge; turn and brown the other side.

Serves 4

*Joe's Crab Shack Crab Cakes

A must have recipe for seafood lovers. Serve as an appetizer with tarter sauce or Dijonaise sauce for dipping.

Ingredients

1 egg yolk
1/3 cup mayonnaise
2 1/2 teaspoons Worcestershire sauce
1 teaspoon lemon juice
1 teaspoon dry mustard
1 teaspoon black pepper
1/4 teaspoon crushed red pepper
1/4 teaspoon Old Bay seasoning
1/4 teaspoon salt
1 1/4 cups fresh bread crumbs
3 tablespoons chopped fresh parsley
1 lb crab meat
flour - to coat

1. Beat together first 9 ingredients.
2. Fold in breadcrumbs and parsley.
3. Fold in crab meat.
4. Form into 4-6 patties.
5. Lightly coat patties in flour on both sides.
6. Deep-fry crab cakes in 350 degrees F oil until browned.

Serves 4-6

*Joe's Crab Shack Étouffée

Ingredients

- 1 teaspoon chopped garlic
- 3/4 cup diced onion
- 1/4 cup diced celery
- 1/2 teaspoon salt
- 1/2 teaspoon cayenne pepper
- 1/2 teaspoon paprika
- 1/4 teaspoon ground mustard seed
- 1/2 teaspoon Worcestershire sauce
- 12 oz. can condensed cream of mushroom soup
- 1/2 cup condensed cream of celery soup
- 1 cup water
- 1/2 lb crawfish meat or 1/2 Lb cubed chicken or 1/2 lb raw, peeled shrimp
- 3 tablespoon sliced green onions
- 1 tablespoon chopped fresh parsley
- 3 cups Rice Pilaf

1. Sauté garlic, onion, celery, and green pepper in butter until soft.
2. Stir in spices, soups, water, and meat of your choice.
3. Bring to simmer and continue cooking until meat is cooked through.
4. Stir in green onion and parsley.
5. Scoop 1/2 cup rice pilaf into center of 6 bowls or soup plates.
6. Pour Étouffée over rice.

Serves 6

*Joe's Crab Shack Rice Pilaf

Ingredients

1 2/3 cups water
1 tablespoon butter
1 bay leaf
1/4 teaspoon white pepper
1 1/3 cups rice
1 teaspoon butter
1/4 cup chopped celery
1/4 cup chopped onion
1/4 cup chopped red bell pepper
1/2 teaspoon minced garlic

1. Bring first 4 ingredients to a boil in a saucepan.
2. Add rice, cover and cook until rice is tender and water is absorbed, about 20 minutes.
3. Sauté celery, onion, peppers, and garlic in butter until tender.
4. Stir sautéed vegetables into rice.

Serves 6

*Joe's Crab Shack Seafood Stuffed Mushrooms

Ingredients

16 large mushroom caps
1 1/4 cup Seafood Stuffing like Joe's Crab Shack's (recipe on next page)
1 cup Alfredo sauce
1/4 cup grated Parmesan cheese
garlic toast for dipping

1. Place mushroom caps (stem side up) in an ovenproof baking dish.
2. Spoon 1 tablespoon hot stuffing into each cap.
3. Pour Alfredo sauce over stuffed mushrooms.
4. Sprinkle Parmesan cheese over top.
5. Broil for 8-10 minutes, or until top is browned.
6. Serve with garlic toast for dipping.

Serves 8

*Joe's Crab Shack Seafood Stuffing

Ingredients

- 1/4 cup margarine
- 1/2 bunch celery - trimmed, diced
- 3 large onions - diced
- 1 1/2 tablespoons minced garlic
- 1/2 lb. Pollock fillets
- 1/2 lb. salad shrimp - chopped
- 1 oz. shrimp base
- 1/4 teaspoon cayenne pepper
- 1/4 teaspoon white pepper
- 2 cups unseasoned croutons
- 1/4 cup seasoned bread crumbs
- 1/2 lb. crab claw meat

1. Sauté celery, onion, and garlic in margarine for until translucent.
2. Add Pollock and cook for 5-7 minutes.
3. Add shrimp and cook for 2 minutes.
4. Drain most (but not all) of liquid from pan.
5. Stir in shrimp base and peppers.
6. Fold in croutons and breadcrumbs.
7. Fold in crab meat.

* *Use this recipe to prepare the Joe's Crab Shack Seafood Stuffed Mushrooms or Stuffed Shrimp Enbrochette's.*

*Joe's Crab Shack Stuffed Shrimp Enbrochette

Ingredients

20 jumbo raw shrimp - peeled, de-veined
1/2 cup Seafood Stuffing like Joe's Crab Shack (see previous recipe)
10 jalapeno slices - halved
2 slices Monterey jack cheese - cut into 20 equal-size pieces
1 lb. raw thin sliced bacon

1. Slice shrimp down the middle of the opposite side you de-veined.
2. Lay shrimp cut side up and press 1 teaspoon prepared stuffing into each shrimp cut.
3. Place a piece of cheese over the stuffing on each shrimp.
4. Wrap each stuffed shrimp in a strip of bacon.
5. Thread 5 shrimp on a bamboo skewer; repeat with remaining shrimp.
6. Deep fry shrimp in 400 degrees F oil until bacon is browned or grill shrimp over a high flame, turning once, until bacon is browned or broil shrimp, turning once, until bacon is browned.

Serves 4

*Junior's Famous No.1 Cheesecake

Commonly known as New York's best cheesecake. It's really that good. Experience this historic dessert from Brooklyn, NY. Junior's cheesecakes can also be ordered online and delivered to your door anywhere in the US - www.JuniorsCheesecake.com.

Thin Sponge Cake Layer for Cheesecake:

Ingredients

1/2 cup cake flour, sifted
1 teaspoon baking powder
pinch of salt
3 extra-large eggs, separated
1/3 cup plus 2 tablespoons granulated sugar
1 teaspoon pure vanilla extract
3 drops pure lemon extract
3 tablespoons unsalted butter, melted
1/4 teaspoon cream of tartar

1. Preheat the oven to 350 degrees F (180 degrees C) and generously butter a 9-inch spring-form pan. Sift the cake flour, baking powder and salt together in a medium-sized bowl and set aside.
2. Beat the egg yolks together in a large bowl with an electric mixer on high speed for 3 minutes. Then, with the mixer still running, gradually add the 1/3 cup of the sugar and continue beating until thick light-yellow ribbons form in the bowl, about 5 minutes more. Beat in the vanilla and lemon extracts.
3. Sift the flour mixture over the batter and stir it in by hand until no more white flecks appear. Then blend in the butter.
4. In a clean bowl, using clean dry beaters, beat the egg whites and cream of tartar together on high speed until frothy.

5. Gradually add the remaining 2 tablespoons sugar and continue beating until stiff peaks form (the whites should stand up in stiff peaks but not be dry). Stir about 1/3 cup of the whites into the batter, then gently fold in the remaining whites - don't worry if a few white specks remain.
6. Gently spoon the batter into the pan. Bake the cake just until the center of the cake springs back when lightly touched, only about 10 minutes (watch carefully). Let the cake cool in the pan on a wire rack while you continue making the cheesecake filling. Do not remove the cake from the pan.

For Cream Cheese Filling:

Ingredients

4 (8-oz.) packages regular cream cheese, at room temperature
1 2/3 cups granulated sugar
1/4 cup cornstarch
1 tablespoon vanilla extract
2 extra large eggs
3/4 cup heavy whipping cream

1. Preheat the oven to 350*F (180*C) and generously butter a 9-inch spring-form pan. Make the batter for the sponge cake as the recipe directs. Evenly spread the batter on the bottom of the pan and bake just until set and golden, about 10 minutes. Place the cake on a wire rack to cool (don't remove it from the pan).
2. While the cake cools, make the cream cheese filling: Place one 8-oz. package of the cream cheese, 1/3 cup of the sugar, and the cornstarch in a large bowl. Beat with

an electric mixer on low speed until creamy, about 3 minutes. Then beat in the remaining 3 packages of cream cheese.

3. Increase the mixer speed to high and beat in the remaining 1 1/3 cups of the sugar, and then beat in the vanilla. Blend in the eggs, one at a time, beating the batter well after adding each one. Blend in the heavy cream. At this point mix the filling only until completely blended (just like they do at Junior's). Be careful not to over-mix the batter.
4. Gently spoon the cheese filling on top of the baked sponge cake layer. Place the spring-form pan in a large shallow pan containing hot water that comes about 1-inch up the sides of the pan. Bake the cheesecake until the center barely jiggles when you shake the pan, about 1 hour.
5. Cool the cake on a wire rack for 1 hour. Then cover the cake with plastic wrap and refrigerate until it's completely cold, at least 4 hours or overnight. Remove the sides of the spring-form pan. Slide the cake off the bottom of the pan onto a serving plate. Or if you wish, simply leave the cake on the removable bottom of the pan and place it on a serving plate. If any cake is left over, cover it with plastic wrap and store in the refrigerator.

Serves 12 to 16

*KFC Honey BBQ Wings

Ingredients

2 cups Bullseye BBQ Sauce
3/4 cup honey
1 cup all-purpose flour
1 teaspoon salt
1/2 teaspoon black pepper
20 chicken drummets

1. Combine flour, salt, and black pepper in a dish and coat chicken in flour mixture
2. Heat BBQ sauce and honey in a saucepan. Once warm, reduce heat to simmer.
3. Add oil to deep fryer and heat to 375 degrees F. Fry chicken 6-8 pieces at a time for 15 minutes or until cooked thoroughly.
4. Drain chicken and smother with BBQ sauce mixture.
5. Repeat with remaining chicken.

Serves 5

*KFC Original Recipe Fried Chicken

What's the secret behind Colonel Sanders' famous 11 herbs and spices? To this day his secret recipe has never been revealed leaving curious minds to speculate. I've tried many different combinations, but there was one that came out tasting exactly like the original...

Ingredients

6 cups Crisco cooking oil
1 egg - beaten
2 cups milk
2 cups all-purpose flour
2 teaspoons black pepper
1 1/2 teaspoons Accent Flavor Enhancer
2 frying chickens with skin - cut each into 6 pieces
3 1/2 tablespoons salt

1. Pour the oil into a pressure fryer and heat on medium to about 400 degrees F.
2. Combine the egg and milk in a bowl.
3. In a different bowl, combine the remaining 4 dry ingredients.
4. Dip the chicken into the egg & milk until fully moistened.
5. Roll the moistened chicken in the flour mixture until completely smothered.
6. Drop in 4 pieces of chicken into the oil and lock the lid in place. Be careful not to burn yourself with the hot oil.
7. Cook for 10 minutes or until thoroughly cooked.
8. Once cooked, release the pressure according to manufacturer's instructions and remove the chicken to paper towels or metal rack to drain.
9. Repeat with the remaining chicken.

Makes 12 pieces

RecipeSecrets.net tip:
Make sure the oil is at 400 degrees F before frying chicken. To avoid making a mess, use utensils when dipping chicken. Quickly lock the lid on the pressure fryer once all pieces of chicken have been added.

*Macaroni Grill Insalata Florentine

Fully loaded salad with spinach, orzo pasta, grilled chicken, sun dried tomatoes, capers, pine nuts, black olives, garlic lemon vinaigrette and Parmesan.

Ingredients

3 oz. julienne-shredded fresh spinach
3 oz. grilled chicken, sliced & chilled
1 oz. ripe Roma tomatoes, diced
1/2 oz. pine nuts, lightly toasted
1/2 oz. sun-dried tomatoes, julienne cut
1/2 oz. capers
1/2 oz. sliced black olives
1/2 oz. julienne-cut radicchio
5 oz. orzo pasta, cooked and chilled
3 oz. roasted, garlic lemon vinaigrette
1/4 oz. shaved Grana Padana Parmesan
fresh cracked pepper, for garnish

1. In the order listed, place all ingredients, except Parmesan cheese, in a chilled mixing bowl.
2. Toss and serve in a bowl. Garnish with shaved Parmesan cheese and fresh cracked pepper.

Serves 4

*Macaroni Grill Pasta Gamberetie E Pinoli

Shrimp, mushrooms, pine nuts, spinach & lemon butter with pasta. Retail price - $12.99 per plate. Our version of this recipe serves 2.

Ingredients

2 tablespoons unsalted butter
4 tablespoons chilled unsalted butter
2 teaspoons garlic, minced
12 medium shrimp, peeled and de-veined
1/4 cup dry white wine
1/2 cup heavy cream
1/3 cup fresh-squeezed lemon juice
Salt and white pepper, to taste
2 tablespoons plain dry bread crumbs
5 1/2 cups fresh spinach, washed
1 (6-oz.) box angel-hair pasta
1 tablespoon toasted pine nuts

1. In a large non-reactive skillet, melt 2 tablespoons butter over medium-high heat. Add the garlic and sauté for about 30 seconds.
2. Add the shrimp and sauté about 30 seconds or until the shrimp is just half cooked.
3. Add the wine and, using a wooden spoon, stir to loosen any brown bits on the bottom of the pan. Let cook 2 minutes, stirring, to finish cooking the shrimp and reduce the liquid. Remove the shrimp to a warm plate and cover with foil.
4. Add the heavy cream to the pan and let cook 3 minutes to reduce. Stir in the lemon juice. Remove the pan from the heat and add the remaining chilled butter, 1 tablespoon at a time, stirring in the next piece after the one before it has just melted.

5. Season with the salt and pepper and stir in the bread crumbs. Return the pan to the heat, add the spinach and cook, stirring,
   1-1/2 minutes or just until the spinach has wilted.
6. Add the shrimp and stir to coat and heat through.
7. To serve, divide the angel-hair pasta between two warmed serving dishes or bowls. Arrange the shrimp on top, spoon the remaining contents of the pan equally over the tops and sprinkle with the pine nuts.

To toast the pine nuts:

1. Spread nuts in a single layer on a baking pan and bake in a preheated 350°F oven 6-8 minutes or until slightly browned. Shake the pan once or twice to toast the nuts evenly.

Serves 2

*Macaroni Grill Roasted Garlic Lemon Vinaigrette

Ingredients

1/4 cup red wine vinegar
3 tablespoons honey
1/2 teaspoon salt
1/2 ounce roasted garlic
3/4 cup virgin olive oil
1/2 lemon, juiced

1. Place vinegar, honey, salt and roasted garlic in a food processor. Puree until garlic is chopped very fine.
2. With the food processor still running, add olive oil and lemon juice.
3. Refrigerate until ready to use.

Serves 2-4

*Macaroni Grill Sesame Shrimp

Ingredients

1/2 ounce olive oil
1/4 cup diced carrots
1/4 cup diced onions
1/4 cup diced celery
1/2 cup diced mushrooms
6 large shrimp (16 to 20 count)
1 teaspoon toasted sesame seeds
1 ounce soy sauce
1 ounce white wine

1. Saute carrots, onions, celery and mushrooms in the oil on medium heat until soft.
2. Add the shrimp and cook for 2 to 3 minutes.
3. Add sesame seeds, soy sauce and white wine.
4. Stir to combine, then serve.

Serves 1-2

*Macaroni Grill Shrimp Portofino

Ingredients

16 medium mushrooms
2 teaspoons chopped garlic
1/2 cup butter, melted
16 large shrimp, cleaned
1/2 teaspoon pepper
3 cloves fresh garlic, crushed, peeled, minced
1/4 cup fresh lemon juice
1 jar marinated artichoke hearts
4 slices lemon
2 tablespoons parsley

1. Saute mushrooms and garlic in butter until almost tender.
2. Add shrimp and saute until shrimp is cooked, about 3 minutes. Be careful not to over cook the shrimp.
3. Add the rest of the ingredients except lemon and parsley and heat through.
4. Serve over pasta or rice. Garnish with lemon slices and parsley.

Serves 4

*McDonald's Egg McMuffin

Ingredients

1 jumbo egg
1 english muffin
butter
1 slice American cheese
1 slice Canadian bacon
1 "12x12" sheet of wax paper
non stick cooking spray
egg ring, or a biscuit cutter

1. Pre-heat an electric griddle to 275 degrees. Toast your english muffin by laying both sides face down on the griddle and applying pressure for about 1 minute. Set aside.
2. Lay your egg ring on the pre-heated grill. Spray with cooking spray. Crack the egg and pour into egg ring on the grill. Break the yolk with a sharp fork.
3. Butter both toasted halves of the english muffin with melted butter. Put a slice of American cheese on the bottom half.
4. About 2 minutes after you started cooking the egg, the whites should firm up. Carefully remove the ring, leaving the egg on the griddle. You may have to "slice" around the edges if it sticks.
5. Very carefully turn the egg over, and lay one slice of Canadian bacon on the griddle. Cook the egg 45 seconds after turning.
6. After about 30 seconds, flip the bacon, and remove the egg, placing it on the bottom half of the english muffin. 30 seconds after flipping the Canadian bacon, remove.
7. Put the Canadian bacon on top of the cooked egg, and cover with the top of the toasted english muffin.

Serves 1

*McDonald's Big Mac

"Two all beef patties, special sauce, lettuce, cheese, pickles, onions on a sesame seed bun."

Ingredients

1 sesame seed hamburger bun
half of an additional hamburger bun
2 100% ground beef patties
dash of salt
1 teaspoon finely diced onion
1/2 cup chopped lettuce
2 slices American cheese
2 to 3 dill pickle slices

Secret Sauce:
1/4 cup Kraft Miracle Whip
1/4 cup mayonnaise
2 tablespoons, heaping, Wishbone deluxe French salad dressing.
1/2 tablespoon Heinz sweet relish
2 teaspoons, heaping, Vlasic dill pickle relish
1 teaspoon sugar
1 teaspoon dried, minced onion
1 teaspoon white vinegar
1 teaspoon ketchup
1/8 teaspoon salt

1. Mix secret sauce ingredients well in a small container. Microwave for 25 seconds and stir again. Cover, and refrigerate for 1 hour before using.
2. Cut the top off of the additional hamburger bun leaving behind a flat bun to be used as the middle section for the Big Mac.
3. Cook hamburger patties in pan on medium high until done. Add salt to taste.
4. Spread the sauce on both sides of the middle bun. Stack the burger as follows: bottom bun, burger, additional ingredients, middle bun, burger, additional ingredients, top bun.

Makes 1 hamburger

*Olive Garden Breadsticks

Ingredients

1 loaf frozen unbaked bread
Pam or cooking oil
Garlic powder
Dry oregano leaf

1. Allowing bread to thaw at room temperature in a greased large mixing bowl.
2. When bread is soft enough to knead, break off pieces and shape into cigar-sized pieces.
3. Place these 3" apart on Pam-sprayed cookie sheets. Let rise in a warm place till doubled - about 1-1/4 hours.
4. Holding can of Pam about 8" from bread sticks, lightly spray top of each and dust with garlic powder.
5. Bake at 375 F - about 20 - 25 minutes or until golden brown.
6. Cool in pan on rack a few minutes before serving.

Serves 4-6

*Olive Garden Bruschetta al Pomodoro

Ingredients

4 medium tomatoes
6 to 8 fresh basil leaves, chopped
8 slices crusty bread
3 cloves garlic
6 tablespoons extra virgin olive oil
Salt, to taste
Pepper, to taste

1. Chop tomatoes, season with salt, pepper, chopped basil and oil.
2. Grill the bread lightly, then brush with garlic and top with tomatoes.

Serves 2

*Olive Garden Fettuccine Alfredo

Ingredients

1 1/2 cups white milk
1 1/2 cups heavy cream
1/2 cup imported Parmesan cheese - grated
1/2 cup imported Romano cheese - grated
6 egg yolks, fresh jumbo eggs
salt and black pepper
1/2 teaspoon parsley
1 teaspoon garlic powder
6 oz. dried fettuccine

1. Heat the milk and cream in a heavy bottom saucepan until it comes to a simmer.
2. Slowly whip in the cheeses and then remove from heat.
3. In a separate bowl, place the egg yolks and slowly whip in a portion of the hot milk and cream mixture.
4. Slowly add the egg yolk mixture back into the remaining cream mixture.
5. Season to taste with the salt and fresh cracked black pepper.
6. Cook fettuccine according to package directions.

7. Add cooked fettuccine to saucepan. Sprinkle in garlic powder and stir until the sauce thickens to the desired consistency.
8. Sprinkle with parsley flakes. Serve immediately.

Serves 6

*Olive Garden Lasagna

Ingredients

1/4 cup butter or margarine
1/4 cup all-purpose flour
2 cups milk
1/4 cup oil-packed sun-dried tomatoes - minced
1 tablespoon minced garlic
3 1/2 cups ricotta cheese
3 eggs
1 cup grated Parmesan cheese
1/2 cup grated Romano cheese
1/2 teaspoon salt
1 teaspoon black pepper
12 lasagna noodles
4 cups shredded mozzarella cheese
1 cup Fontina cheese
Marinara/spaghetti sauce - to top

RecipeSecrets.net tip: Fontina cheese, made from cow's milk, is a firm, creamy, delicate Italian cheese with a slightly nutty taste. You may have to go to an Italian market to get fine Fontina Cheese.

1. Melt butter over medium heat in 1 quart saucepan.
2. Add flour and stir until well-blended; cook until frothy.
3. Add milk, stirring constantly with wire whisk as mixture comes to a simmer.
4. Cook and stir until thickened (3-4 minutes).
5. Drain and mince tomatoes and place in 3 quart mixing bowl.
6. Add garlic, ricotta, eggs, Parmesan, Romano, salt, and pepper to bowl.
7. Add 1 1/2 cups of cooled cream sauce and mix until well blended.

8. Place 3 lasagna noodles in a 9" X 13" X 2" lightly oiled baking dish, overlapping slightly.
9. Spread 1 1/2 cups cheese filling over noodles; sprinkle with one cup mozzarella and 1/4 cup fontina cheese.
10. Repeat pasta and cheese layering three more times; top with remaining three lasagna noodles.
11. Spread 1/2 cup of reserved cream sauce over top and cover lightly with aluminum foil.
12. Bake in a 350 degrees F oven for 1 hour.
13. Remove from oven and keep warm at least 30 minutes before serving.
14. Serve topped with hot marinara and Parmesan cheese.

Serves 5

*Olive Garden Oven Roasted Potatoes

Ingredients

2 medium baking potatoes
4 tablespoons olive oil
1 medium green pepper
1 medium red pepper
1/2 teaspoon salt
2 teaspoons fresh rosemary, chopped
1 teaspoon fresh garlic, minced
4 teaspoons fresh parsley, chopped
1/2 cup Romano cheese, grated

1. Preheat oven to 350 degrees F.
2. Peel potatoes and dice into1/2-inch pieces. Core and seed peppers and dice into1/2-inch pieces. Set aside.
3. Mix olive oil, rosemary, salt and pepper in a bowl.
4. In a small baking pan, toss potatoes and peppers with the oil and herb mixture. Bake for 10 minutes or until potatoes are fork tender.
5. Sprinkle potatoes with parsley and Romano cheese.

Serves 2

*Olive Garden Pasta e Fagioli

Ingredients

3 teaspoons oil
2 pounds ground beef
12 oz. onion - chopped
14 oz. carrots - sliced thinly
14 oz. celery - diced
48 oz. canned tomatoes - diced
2 cups cooked red kidney beans
2 cups cooked white kidney beans
80 oz. beef stock
3 teaspoons oregano
2 teaspoons pepper
5 teaspoons parsley - chopped
1 1/2 teaspoon tabasco sauce
48 oz. spaghetti sauce
8 oz. dry pasta shell macaroni

1. Sauté beef in oil in large 10 quart pot until beef starts to brown. Add onions, carrots, celery and tomatoes and simmer for about 10 minutes.
2. Drain and rinse beans and add to the pot. Also add beef stock, oregano, pepper, Tabasco, spaghetti sauce, and noodles.
3. Add chopped parsley. Simmer until celery and carrots are tender (about 45 minutes).

Makes 9 quarts of soup.

Serves 10

*Olive Garden Pizza Bianco

Ingredients

2 seasoned thick 6-inch diameter pizza crusts, ready-to-serve

Cheese Filling
1/2 cup ricotta
1/4 cup grated Parmesan cheese
1/4 cup shredded mozzarella cheese
1/4 cup shredded Fontina cheese
1 tablespoon minced yellow onions
1 1/2 tablespoons milk
1/4 teaspoon salt

Toppings
1/4 cup sliced green onions
1/3 cup diced black olives
1/3 cup seeded chopped tomatoes
1/2 cup grated mozzarella cheese
1 pinch oregano, or to taste
1 pinch basil, or to taste

1. Combine all ingredients for the filling and mix thoroughly.
2. Divide the filling in half and spread on each crust.
3. Prepare toppings and divide in half. Sprinkle green onions, olives and tomatoes over crusts.
4. Top with mozzarella and Parmesan.
5. Bake in a 375 degree F oven for 8 to 10 minutes until filling is hot and cheese has melted.
6. Cut into 6 wedges.

Makes 2 Small Pizzas

*Olive Garden Pork Filettino

This recipe goes great with Olive Gardens Oven Roasted Potatoes.

Ingredients

4 pork tenderloins
8 tablespoons extra-virgin olive oil
4 tablespoons fresh garlic, minced
4 tablespoons fresh rosemary, chopped
1/2 teaspoon salt
1/2 teaspoon black pepper
1 package or jar prepared veal demi-glaze

1. Season tenderloin with salt and pepper on all sides.
2. Brush with olive oil, rosemary, garlic and parsley. Let marinate approximately two hours.
3. Cook on a hot grill until internal temperature reaches 165 degrees F.
4. Heat demi-glaze and pour over pork. Garnish with fresh rosemary.

Serves 4

*Olive Garden Salad Dressing

Ingredients

1/2 cup distilled white vinegar
1 teaspoon lemon juice
2 tablespoons beaten egg
1/3 cup water
1/3 cup vegetable oil
1/4 cup corn syrup
3 tablespoons grated Romano cheese
2 tablespoons dry, unflavored pectin (optional)
1 1/4 teaspoons salt
1/2 teaspoon minced garlic
1/4 teaspoon dried parsley
1 pinch dried oregano
1 pinch red pepper flakes

1. Mix all the ingredients in a blender on low for about 30 seconds.
2. Chill in refrigerator for 90 minutes.
3. Serve over your favorite salad.

Makes 1 1/2 cups

*Olive Garden Sangria

Sangria is a refreshing party drink that was created in Spain. Every restaurant has its own twist to this fruit filled drink. We selected this one for its unique taste. Sangria's appeal is all about taking your favorite red wine, your favorite fruits, and experimenting with them.

Ingredients

1.5 liters of dry Red Wine
10 oz. Grenadine
16 oz. cranberry juice cocktail
12 oz. sweet vermouth
10 oz. sugar water
(5 oz sugar diluted)
strawberries
oranges
crushed ice

1. Mix all ingredients except for ice in a nice size pitcher. Pour sangria in glass and then add ice.
2. Serve each glass with fruit

Makes 1 gallon.

*Olive Garden Tiramisu Dessert

Ingredients

1 Sponge cake (10-12 inch) -- About 3" tall
3 oz Strong black coffee -- or Instant espresso
3 oz Brandy or rum
1 1/2 lb Cream cheese or mascarpone at room temperature
1 1/2 c superfine/powdered sugar
Unsweetened cocoa powder

1. Cut across middle of sponge cake forming two layers, each about 1 1/2 inches high.
2. Blend coffee and brandy. Sprinkle enough of mixture over bottom half of cake to flavor it strongly.
3. Don't moisten cake too much or it may collapse on serving. Beat room-temperature cheese and 1 cup sugar until sugar is completely dissolved and cheese is light and spreadable. Test for sweetness during beating, adding more sugar if needed.
4. Spread cut surface of bottom layer with half of the cheese mixture.
5. Replace second layer and top this with remaining cheese mixture.
6. Sprinkle top liberally with sifted cocoa.
7. Refrigerate cake for at least 2 hours before cutting and serving.

Makes 1 Cake

*Outback Steakhouse Honey Wheat Bushman Bread

Ingredients

1 1/2 cups water - warmed
2 tablespoons butter - softened
1/2 cup honey
2 cups bread flour
2 cups wheat flour
1 tablespoon cocoa
1 tablespoon sugar
2 teaspoons instant coffee
1 teaspoon salt
2 1/4 teaspoons yeast
1 teaspoon caramel color (optional)
3 tablespoons cornmeal - for dusting

1. Place all of the ingredients in the bread machine and process on dough setting. The dough will be a little on the wet side and sticky, but if it seems too wet add more flour. When dough is done let it rise for 1 hour.
2. Remove from pan, punch down and divide into 8 portions. Form portions into tubular shaped loaves about 6-8 inches long and 2 inches wide.
3. Sprinkle the entire surface of the loaves with cornmeal and place them on 2 cookie sheets. Cover and let rise for 1 hour.
4. Bake at 350 degrees F for 20-25 minutes. Serve warm with whipped butter.

Makes 1 Loaf

*Outback Steakhouse Key Lime Pie

Ingredients

Filling

- 1 water
- 3 c sugar
- 1 pk unflavored gelatin
- 1 salt
- 3 limes , juice of
- 1 condensed milk

Crust

- 1 butter
- 1 graham cracker crumbs

1. To prepare the filling, heat water, sugar, gelatin, salt and lime juice in pot but do not boil.
2. Then mix in condensed milk and heat again without boiling.
3. To prepare the crust, place butter in a pan and melt.
4. Mix in crumbs until it makes a crust-like substance.
5. Pour filling into crust and let cool.

Makes 1 Pie

*Outback Steakhouse Marinated Steak

Ingredients

4 beef steaks
1 cup beer
1 tablespoon packed brown sugar
1 teaspoon seasoned salt
1/2 teaspoon black pepper
1/2 teaspoon onion powder
1/2 teaspoon garlic powder

1. Place your favorite cut of steak in a shallow pan, pour beer over, and marinate for 1 hour in refrigerator.
2. Remove steak from beer.
3. Combine dry ingredients and rub over steaks.
4. Allow to marinate for 30 minutes in refrigerator.
5. Preheat a grill to medium high heat.
6. Grill steaks over a medium-high flame until desired doneness.

Serves 4

*Panda Express Orange Flavored Chicken

Tender, juicy chicken pieces lightly battered and fried, sautéed in a sweet and mildly spicy chili sauce with scallions.

Ingredients

1 lb. chicken breast meat
1 egg white
1 teaspoon salt
1 teaspoon sugar
4 cups vegetable oil to be used for frying
1 cup cornstarch

Orange Sauce
1 cup water
1/2 cup ketchup
1/2 cup sugar
1/8 cup vinegar
1 tablespoon soy sauce
4 teaspoons cornstarch
2 teaspoons sesame oil
2 tablespoons vegetable oil
1 tablespoon grated orange peel
2 tablespoons chopped scallion

1. Cut chicken breast into 1/2-inch cubes, set aside.
2. To make marinade - combine egg white, salt and sugar in a bowl and stir vigorously until ingredients are thoroughly mixed. Add chicken cubes to marinade and stir to coat well.
3. To make orange sauce - combine water, ketchup, sugar, vinegar, soy sauce, 4 teaspoons cornstarch and sesame oil; stir and set aside. Place a pot over high heat. When pot is hot, add the 2 tablespoons vegetable oil and heat. Add orange peel and scallion and stir for about 20 seconds, taking care not to burn the orange peel.
4. Pour combined sauce ingredients into the pot and cook, stirring frequently, until sauce has thickened, about 12-15 minutes.

5. Preheat 4 cups oil to 350-375°F. Meanwhile, put marinated chicken in the plastic baggie containing the cornstarch. Shake chicken well for about 20 seconds or until chicken is covered with cornstarch. Shake off all excess cornstarch and fry chicken in hot oil until golden brown, approximately 2 1/2 minutes. Remove chicken from oil with a slotted spoon, drain well and set aside. Add fried chicken to pot with heated orange sauce, stir for about 30 seconds, then serve immediately.
6. Serve with steamed rice.

Serves 4

*PF Chang Chicken Lettuce Wrap

Quickly cooked spiced chicken served with cool lettuce cups. Makes a great appetizer.

Ingredients

8 dried shiitake mushrooms
1 teaspoon cornstarch
2 teaspoons dry sherry
2 teaspoons water
salt and pepper
1 1/2 lbs. boneless, skinless chicken
5 teaspoons oil
1 teaspoon fresh minced ginger
2 cloves garlic, minced
2 green onions, minced
2 small dried chiles (optional)
8 oz. bamboo shoots, minced
8 oz. water chestnuts, minced
1 package cellophane Chinese rice noodles, prepared according to package

Cooking Sauce

1 teaspoon Hoisin sauce
1 teaspoon soy sauce
1 teaspoon dry sherry
2 teaspoons oyster sauce
2 teaspoons water
1 teaspoon sesame oil
1 teaspoon sugar
2 teaspoons cornstarch
Iceberg or Bibb lettuce leaves

1. Cover mushrooms with boiling water, let stand 30 minutes then drain.
2. Cut and discard woody stems. Mince mushrooms. Set aside.
3. Mix all ingredients for cooking sauce in bowl, and set aside.
4. In medium bowl, combine cornstarch, sherry water, soy sauce, salt, pepper and chicken. Stir to coat chicken thoroughly.
5. Stir in 1 teaspoon oil and let sit 15 minutes to marinate.

6. Heat wok or large skillet over medium high heat.
7. Add 3 tablespoons oil, then add chicken and stir fry for about 3-4 minutes. Set aside.
8. Add 2 tablespoons oil to pan.
9. Add ginger, garlic, chiles (if desired), and onion; stir fry about a minute or so.
10. Add mushrooms, bamboo shoots and water chestnuts; stir fry an additional 2 minutes. Return chicken to pan.
11. Add mixed cooking sauce to pan. Cook until thickened and hot.
12. Break cooked cellophane noodles into small pieces, and cover bottom of serving dish with them. Then pour chicken mixture on top of noodles. Spoon into lettuce leaf and roll.

Serves 4-6

*PF Chang Chicken with Black Bean Sauce

Slices of chicken, stir-fried in black bean sauce.

Ingredients

4 whole chicken breasts
1 teaspoon fresh minced ginger
2 teaspoons fermented black beans
3 teaspoons minced scallions (white part only)
4 oz. Peking Stir Fry sauce (see recipe below)
12 oz. unseasoned chicken stock
1/2 teaspoon minced garlic
1/2 teaspoon sugar
dash of white pepper

Peking Stir Fry Sauce
1/2 cup water
2 teaspoons Shaohsing wine or sherry
2 teaspoons mushroom soy sauce
2 teaspoons oyster sauce
1 teaspoon sugar
1 teaspoon cornstarch

1. Cut whole chicken breasts in half so you have 8 breast filets. Cut all breast filets on a bias. Marinate with one egg, 2 tablespoons canola oil and 1 tablespoon cornstarch.
2. Heat wok until hot. Add oil, then chicken and cook until opaque all over.
3. Strain and remove excess oil from wok.
4. Add ginger, scallion and stir fry. Add chicken and garlic. Then add Peking stir fry sauce and add chicken stock. Add sugar, then a dash of white pepper.
5. Thicken with a thin paste of cornstarch and water to your liking.
6. Peking Stir Fry Sauce Mix ingredients together until cornstarch is incorporated. Stir well before using.

Serves 4

*Planet Hollywood Captain Crunch Chicken

Another great theme restaurant focusing on movie and Hollywood memorabilia. This unique dish actually uses cereal breaded against the chicken to make it tasty and crunchy.

Ingredients

2 cups Captain Crunch Cereal, crushed
1 1/2 cups Corn Flakes, crushed
1 egg
1 cup milk
1 cup all-purpose flour
1 teaspoon onion powder
1 teaspoon garlic powder
1/2 teaspoon black pepper
2 pounds Chicken breast - boneless, skinless, cut into chicken tenders (long slices)
vegetable oil for frying

1. Beat the egg with milk and set aside.
2. Stir together the flour, onion and garlic powders and black pepper. Set aside.
3. Dip chicken pieces into the seasoned flour. Move around to coat well, then shake off the excess flour. Dip into the egg wash, coating well, then dip into the cereal mixture, coating well.
4. Heat oil in a large heavy skillet to 325 degrees F.
5. Drop coated chicken tenders carefully into the hot oil and cook until golden brown and fully cooked, 3 to 5 minutes depending on size.
6. Drain and serve with Creole mustard sauce.

Serves 2

*Planet Hollywood The Terminator

A popular alcoholic drink at this restaurant chain. It's very strong but it goes down smooth. Please drink responsibly.

Ingredients

1/2 oz vodka
1/2 oz white rum
1/2 oz gin
1/2 oz Grand Marnier
1/2 oz Kahlua
2 oz sweet & sour mix
1 oz cranberry juice
1 splash beer

1. Combine crushed ice with all ingredients, except beer, in a tumbler. Shake.
2. Pour a splash of beer on top and serve with a straw.

Makes 1 serving

*Popeyes Cajun Rice

Ingredients

1 lb. lean ground beef
1/2 cup finely diced bell pepper
1/3 cup diced green onions
1/2 teaspoon garlic powder
1/2 teaspoon celery flakes
1 teaspoon Creole seasoning
1/4 teaspoon red pepper
4 cups long grain rice cooked and drained
1/4 - 1/3 cup water
1/4 teaspoon black pepper

RecipeSecrets.net tip: For a serious Cajun experience, add more Creole seasoning and red pepper. To get the best results, use good quality rice for this recipe. Just follow the directions on your selected rice brand to prepare.

1. In frying pan stir in ground beef, bell pepper and cook on medium high heat until beef looses its pink color and bell pepper is soft.
2. Remove excess grease.
3. Turn temperature down to medium or medium low.
4. Add remaining ingredients, stir and cook together until ground beef is completely cooked and liquid is gone about 25 - 35 min.

Serves 4-6

*Popeyes Dirty Rice

Ingredients

1 lb spicy bulk breakfast sausage
1 can clear chicken broth - (14 oz.)
1/2 cup long-grain rice
1 teaspoon dry minced onion

1. Brown sausage in skillet until pink color disappears, crumbling with fork.
2. Stir in broth, rice and minced onion.
3. Simmer gently, covered, 18 to 20 minutes or until rice is tender and most of broth is absorbed.

Serves 4

*Popeyes Fried Chicken

Ingredients

3 cups self-rising flour
1 cup cornstarch
3 tablespoons seasoned salt
2 tablespoons paprika
1 teaspoon baking soda
1 package Italian salad dressing mix - powder
1 package onion soup mix - (1 1/2 oz.)
1 package spaghetti sauce mix - (1/2 oz.)
3 tablespoons sugar
3 cups corn flakes - crush slightly
2 eggs - well beaten
1/4 cup cold water
4 lbs. chicken - cut up

1. Combine first 9 ingredients in large bowl. Put the cornflakes into another bowl. Put eggs and water in a 3rd bowl.
2. Put enough corn oil into a heavy roomy skillet to fill it 1" deep. Heat skillet.
3. Grease a 9x12x2 baking pan. Set aside.
4. Preheat oven to 350.
5. Dip chicken pieces 1 at a time as follows: 1-Into dry coating mix. 2-Into egg and water mix. 3-Into corn flakes. 4-Then back into dry mix. 5-Drop into hot oil, skin-side-down and brown 3 to 4 minutes on medium high. Turn and brown other side of each piece.
6. Place chicken in prepared pan in single layer, skin-side-up. Seal in foil, on 3 sides only, leaving 1 side loose for steam to escape.
7. Bake at 350 degrees F for 35-40 minutes removing foil then to test tenderness of chicken. Allow to bake uncovered 5 minutes longer to crisp the coating.

Serves 4

*Red Lobster Batter-Fried Shrimp

Ingredients

1 1/2 pounds shrimp, peeled & de-veined
1/2 cup oil
1 egg, beaten
1 cup all-purpose flour
1/2 cup milk
3/4 teaspoon seasoned salt
1/4 teaspoon salt
oil for deep frying

1. Preheat oil to 350 degrees F. Combine 1/2 cup oil and egg; beat well.
2. Add remaining ingredients except oil for frying and stir until well blended.
3. Dip shrimp into batter to coat. Drop shrimp into hot oil and fry for 30-60 seconds or until golden brown. Remove with slotted spoon; drain on paper towel.

Serves 6

*Red Lobster Cheddar Biscuits

Ingredients

2 cups Bisquick® baking mix
2/3 cup milk
1/2 cup shredded mild cheddar cheese
1/4 cup melted butter
1/4 teaspoon garlic powder
parsley flakes

1. Mix Bisquick, cheddar and milk into soft dough. Beat with a wooden spoon for about 30 seconds.
2. Spoon on to greased cookie sheet. Smooth down tops to avoid hard points from forming.
3. Bake for 8 to 10 min at 450 degrees F.
4. While baking, melt butter in pan and stir in garlic powder.
5. Once biscuits are cooked, brush butter on tops, sprinkle with parsley and serve hot.

Serves 10

*Red Lobster Clam Chowder

Ingredients

1 quart clam juice
1 cup nonfat dry milk powder
1 3/4 cups chicken broth
2/3 cup all-purpose flour
2 stalks celery chopped fine
1 tablespoon minced dry onion
10 oz. can clams drained
1 pinch parsley flakes
2 medium baked potatoes – peeled and crumbled
salt and pepper to taste

1. In blender, puree clam juice, broth, milk powder, and flour.
2. Pour into 2 1/2 quart saucepan and simmer, stirring constantly, over medium-high heat until thick and smooth.
3. Reduce heat to low; stir in celery, onion, clams, parsley, and potatoes.
4. Simmer for 45-60 minutes, then season with salt and pepper.

Serves 6

*Red Lobster Grouper Siciliano

Ingredients

2 pounds skinless fresh grouper fillets
1/2 cup butter
1 clove garlic; crushed
2 cups italian style bread crumbs

1. Cut fillets into serving size pieces.
2. In a shallow saucepan, melt butter; add garlic.
3. Add garlic butter to bread crumbs.
4. Dip fish in crumb mixture. Place on baking sheet.
5. Bake at 450 degrees F, for 10 minutes per inch of thickness or until fish flakes easily when tested with a fork.

Serves 4-6

*Red Lobster Lobster Fondue

Ingredients

1 lb. processed cheese food - cubed
1/2 cup milk
1/2 teaspoon cayenne pepper
1/2 teaspoon paprika
1 lobster tail - boiled
1/2 cup chopped red bell pepper
2 tablespoons fresh minced parsley

1. Combine all ingredients except red pepper and parsley in a saucepan.
2. Heat on medium-low heat, stirring constantly, until cheese has melted.
3. When ready to serve, garnish with red bell pepper and parsley.

Serves 8

*Red Lobster Roasted Maine Lobster with Crabmeat Stuffing

Ingredients

Stuffing
1 pound blue crab meat
1 teaspoon shallot, minced
1 teaspoon parsley
1 tablespoon mayonnaise
1 tablespoon bread crumbs
1 whole egg
1 teaspoon lemon juice
1/8 teaspoon Worcestershire

Lobster
2 whole 1 1/4 pound Maine lobsters
1 stick butter, cut into pieces
1 teaspoon paprika
2 tablespoons lemon juice

Preparation - Stuffing

1. Blend all ingredients except crab.
2. Fold in crab meat, refrigerate

Preparation - Lobsters

1. Split lobsters lengthwise with a large knife, remove stomach sac.
2. Place equal portions of crab stuffing in each head.
3. Crack claws with the blunt side of knife.
4. Pour lemon juice on tail meat, then sprinkle with paprika and dot with pieces of butter.
5. Bake in a 400°F oven for 15 minutes.
6. Serve with melted butter and lemon wedges.

Serves 2

*Red Lobster Shrimp Diablo

Ingredients

3 lbs. large, uncooked, unpeeled shrimp
milk for soaking
1 cup unsalted butter
1 jar Kraft BBQ Sauce
1/2 cup catsup
1/4 cup hot sauce
1 tablespoon ground black pepper

1. Wash shrimp in cool water and remove heads if needed.
2. Soak shrimp in milk overnight.
3. Mix sauces and pepper in a sauce pan and stir until boiling.
4. Remove from heat and refrigerate for at least four hours.
5. Drain milk from shrimp, place them in a baking pan, and cover evenly with the sauce. Let stand 1 hour.
6. Bake uncovered in a 450 degrees F oven for 15 minutes (less time for smaller shrimp).

Serves 6

*Red Lobster South Beach Seafood Paella

Ingredients

6 tablespoon olive oil
1 cup minced onions
1 small sweet red bell pepper, seeded, cut into 1/2" pieces
1 small sweet green bell pepper, seeded, cut into 1/2" pieces
1 cup canned chopped tomatoes, drained
1 tablespoon minced garlic
1 tablespoon minced fresh thyme
1 lb. sea scallops
sea salt and freshly ground black pepper
6 oz. andouille sausage, cut into 1/2" thick pieces
1/2 cup dry white wine
3 cups long-grain rice
1 teaspoon saffron threads
3 cups chicken stock, hot
3 cups clam juice, hot
12 large or jumbo shrimp, cleaned and peeled, leaving tails intact
1 lb. fresh fish (grouper, scrod, haddock, halibut or swordfish), skinless, cut into 1" chunks
16 fresh mussels
1/2 lb. sugar snap peas
1 medium red pepper, cut into long 1/2" wide strips
chopped fresh parsley to garnish

1. In a heavy 12" skillet, heat 3 tablespoons olive oil until hot. Add the onions and pepper, and cook, stirring for 5 minutes until they're soft and transparent.
2. Add tomatoes, garlic and thyme. Cook, stirring for 5 more minutes, until most of the liquid in the pan evaporates and the mixture is thick.
3. Put the sofrito aside for later.

Seafood and Sausage:

1. Season the fish, shrimp and scallops with salt and pepper.

2. In a skillet, heat 3 tablespoons of olive oil over moderately high heat until hot.
3. Add the fish, shrimp and scallops, as well as the mussels, and sauté for 3-5 minutes.
4. Add the sausage and cook until light brown.
5. Transfer to a plate and deglaze pan with 1/2 cup of dry white wine.

Paella:

1. About 30 minutes before you plan to serve the paella, preheat an oven to 400 degrees F.
2. In a 14" paella pan or shallow casserole dish at least 14" in diameter, combine the sofrito, rice and saffron.
3. Pour in 3 cups of chicken stock and 2 cups of clam juice (save 1 cup for the end). Stirring constantly, bring to a boil over high heat.
4. Remove the pan from the heat immediately and season with salt and pepper.
5. Arrange the seafood on the top of the rice.
6. Set the pan on the lowest shelf in the oven and bake uncovered for 20 minutes. Do not stir the paella once it goes in the oven.
7. Sprinkle the sugar snap peas and the red pepper strips over the whole paella, and bake for 5-10 minutes more, or until all of the liquid has been absorbed by the rice and the grains are tender, but not too soft. If the rice needs to be softer, add the remaining cup of clam juice.
8. Remove from stove and let stand for five minutes before serving. Garnish with parsley.

Serves 4-6

*Ruby Tuesday Chicken Quesadillas

This restaurant was formed in 1972, when Sandy Beall and four of his fraternity buddies from the University of Tennessee opened the first restaurant adjacent to the college campus in Knoxville. Today Ruby Tuesday is one of three large public companies that dominate the bar-and-grill category of casual dining.

Ingredients

5 oz. boned, skinned chicken breast halves
Italian salad dressing - to coat
1 12" flour tortilla
margarine - melted, for coating
1 cup shredded Monterey Jack/Cheddar cheese
1 tablespoon diced tomato
1 tablespoon diced jalapeno pepper
Cajun seasoning - to taste
1/2 cup shredded lettuce
1/4 cup diced tomato
sour cream - low fat okay
salsa - for dipping

1. Place chicken breast in a bowl with enough Italian dressing to coat; allow to marinate 30 minutes in refrigerator.
2. Grill marinated chicken until done in a lightly oiled pan. Cut into 3/4" pieces and set aside.
3. Brush one side of tortilla with margarine and place in frying pan over medium heat.

4. On one half of tortilla, add (in order) cheese, 1 tablespoon tomatoes, peppers, and Cajun seasoning. Spread evenly and then top with diced chicken. Fold empty tortilla side to close and flip over in pan so that cheese is on top of chicken. Cook until cheese melts.
5. Remove from pan to serving plate and cut into six equal wedges. Serve with the lettuce, 1/4 cup tomatoes, sour cream and salsa on the side of the same plate.

Serves 4

*Ruby Tuesday Sonoran Chicken Pasta

Ingredients

6 oz. boneless, skinless chicken breast, grilled and sliced into 1/4 inch slices
10 oz. penne pasta, cooked
3/4 cup Sonoran cheese sauce
1/3 cup spicy black beans (optional)
1/4 cup diced tomatoes for garnish
1 teaspoon green onion, sliced (optional)

Sonoran Cheese Sauce:
6 tablespoons butter or margarine
1/2 cup onion, finely chopped
1 small clove garlic, minced
1/3 cup all purpose flour
1 cup hot water
1 tablespoon chicken stock paste
1 cup half-and-half
1/2 teaspoon sugar
1/4 teaspoon hot sauce
1 teaspoon lemon juice
1/4 teaspoon cayenne pepper
3/4 cup shredded parmesan cheese
3/4 cup Velveeta cheese
3/4 cup prepared salsa
1/2 cup sour cream
salt and pepper to taste

1. Place pasta into mixing bowl. Add cheese sauce and toss to coat evenly. Pour into heated bowl. Place chicken on top of pasta then ladle black beans on top. Sprinkle with diced tomatoes and chopped green onions.

Sonoran Cheese Sauce:

1. Melt butter or margarine in a saucepan and add onion and garlic.
2. Saute until onion is transparent.
3. Stir in flour to make roux and cook for 5 minutes stirring often.

4. Mix the hot water, chicken stock and half and half.
5. Add mixture slowly to roux, stirring constantly.
6. Allow to cook 5 minutes (sauce should have the consistency of honey). Add salt, sugar, hot sauce, lemon juice, cayenne, and parmesan cheese to sauce. Stir to blend. Do not allow to boil. Add Velveeta to sauce and stir until melted. Add salsa and sour cream to sauce and blend.

Makes 5 cups

*Sara Lee Original Cream Cheesecake

Ingredients

1-9 inch graham cracker crust

Filling:
16 oz cream cheese
1 cup sour cream
2 tablespoons cornstarch
1 cup granulated sugar
2 tablespoons butter
1 teaspoon vanilla extract

Topping:
3/4 cup sour cream
1/4 cup powdered sugar

1. For the filing: mix the cream cheese, sour cream, cornstarch, and sugar in the bowl of a mixer. Mix until sugar has dissolved. Add the butter and vanilla, blend until smooth.
2. Pour the filling over the crust. Bake for 30 to 35 minutes, or until a knife inserted 1 inch from the edge comes out clean. Cool for 1 hour.
3. For the topping: mix the sour cream and powdered sugar. Spread the mixture over the top of the cool cheesecake. Chill or freeze until ready to eat.

Makes one 9-inch Pie

*Shoney's Pot Roast

Ingredients

- 2 tablespoons butter or margarine
- 3 lbs. rump roast - trimmed of fat
- 2 stalks celery - chopped
- 1 large onion - chopped
- 3 cloves garlic - minced
- 1/2 teaspoon parsley flakes
- 1/2 tablespoon dried thyme
- 2 cups beef broth
- 20 whole peppercorns
- 1 whole bay leaf
- 1/2 tablespoon salt
- 2 carrots - sliced
- 2 potatoes - peeled, cubed
- 1/2 teaspoon salt
- 1/3 cup all-purpose flour

1. Brown roast in butter in Dutch oven, then remove meat from Dutch oven.
2. Sauté in celery, onion, garlic, parsley, and thyme in Dutch oven for 5 minutes, then return meat to Dutch oven.
3. Add the beef broth, peppercorns, bay leaf, and salt to Dutch oven and bake in a 325 degrees F oven, covered, for 4 hours, basting every 1/2 hour.
4. Remove roast from Dutch oven.
5. Strain stock into bowl; discard vegetables.
6. Using 2 forks, shred roast into bite-size pieces.
7. Pour reserved stock over beef in Dutch oven.
8. Add carrots, potatoes, and salt to Dutch oven and bake in a 325 degrees F oven for 45 minutes.

9. Drain stock from Dutch oven and add enough beef broth to stock to make 3 cups.
10. Whisk stock and flour together in saucepan and simmer until thick.
11. Pour gravy over meat and vegetables.

Serves 8

*Shoney's Tomato Florentine Soup

Ingredients

2 cans clear chicken broth - 14 oz each
1 can sliced stewed tomatoes - (14 oz)
12 oz. V-8 juice
10 oz. cream of tomato soup
1 tablespoon sugar
10 oz. frozen chopped spinach
dash nutmeg
salt and pepper

1. Combine broth, tomatoes, juice and soup in a saucepan with a wire whisk over medium heat.
2. Add remaining ingredients, without even thawing spinach.
3. Allow to heat gently 30 minutes on medium-low until spinach is tender. Keep hot without letting it boil.

Serves 6

*Sizzler Fried Shrimp

Ingredients

1 cup sifted all-purpose flour
1 egg beaten
1/2 cup milk
1 cup dry bread crumbs
1 1/2 teaspoon salt
1/2 teaspoon dried basil
1/2 teaspoon parsley flakes
1/8 teaspoon garlic powder
1/8 teaspoon onion powder
24 raw jumbo shrimp – peeled and deveined

1. Place flour in bowl; set aside.
2. Combine egg and milk in bowl; set aside.
3. Combine remaining dry ingredients in bowl; set aside.
4. Dip shrimp in flour, then in egg mixture, then in bread crumb
   mixture.
5. Deep-fry shrimp in 350 degrees F oil for 3-4 minutes.
6. Drain on brown paper bags.

Serves 4

*Starbuck's Frappuccino

Ingredients

1/2 cup fresh espresso
1/2 cup 2% Milk
1/4 cup granulated sugar
1 tablespoon pectin

1. Combine all of the ingredients in a pitcher or covered container. Stir or shake until sugar is dissolved.
2. Fill a glass with ice and either serve mixture over ice, or pour glass contents into blender and frappe for 30-45 seconds.

Serves 1

*T.G.I. Friday's Baked Potato Skins

T.G.I. Friday's, one of the first American casual dining chains, is a dining experience that has become the favorite pastime of millions since 1965. The first T.G.I. Friday's was located at First Avenue and 63rd Street in New York City. Their focus is on providing a comfortable, relaxing environment where guests can enjoy quality food and have a good time.

Ingredients

10 baked potato skin halves (empty of potato)
1 tablespoon melted butter
seasoned salt
1 tablespoon snipped fresh chives
1/2 cup fried bacon, diced and crispy fried (about 5 strips)
3/4 cup shredded Cheddar cheese

1. Heat oven to 375 degrees F.
2. Brush potato shells with melted butter and sprinkle seasoned salt to taste.
3. Bake for 15 to 20 minutes until crisp but not dry and hard. Remove and sprinkle with cheese, bacon and chives. Place back in oven until cheese is melted.
4. Serve with sour cream.

Serves 4

*T.G.I. Friday's Broccoli Cheese Soup

Ingredients

1 quart water
2 cup diced potatoes
2 chicken bouillon cubes
1 cup diced onion
20 oz. frozen broccoli, chopped or 1 bunch fresh broccoli
2 cans cream of chicken soup
1 lb. Velveeta or American cheese

1. Mix water, potatoes, bouillon, onion and broccoli together. Cook on medium heat until done, about 20-30 minutes.
2. Add soup and cheese. Reduce heat and let simmer for 15 minutes

Serves 2

*T.G.I. Friday's Jack Daniels Dipping Sauce

Ingredients

1/3 cup diced red onions
1/2 teaspoon finely diced garlic
1/2 cup Water
1/2 cup brown sugar
1/3 cup teriyaki sauce
1/4 cup soy sauce
1/3 cup white grape juice
1/2 cup Jack Daniels Black Label bourbon
1/2 teaspoon tabasco sauce

1. Place ingredients in sauce pan in order listed.
2. Mix and stir after each ingredient.
3. Place on medium heat and stir until mixture reaches boiling stage.
4. Reduce temperature to low until mixture is slowly simmering.
5. Cook sauce for 35 - 45 minutes.

Serve and enjoy.

*Taco Bell Burrito Supreme

Ingredients

1 pound lean ground beef
1/4 cup all-purpose flour
1 tablespoon chili powder
1 teaspoon salt
1/2 teaspoon dried minced onion
1/2 teaspoon paprika
1/4 teaspoon onion powder
dash garlic powder
1/2 cup water
1 16-oz. can refried beans
8 10-inch flour tortillas
1/2 cup enchilada sauce
3/4 cup sour cream
2 cups shredded lettuce
2 cups shredded cheddar cheese
1 medium tomato, diced
1/2 cup diced yellow onion

1. In a medium bowl, combine the first 8 ingredients. Thoroughly massage the ingredients into the ground beef using your hands.
2. Add the seasoned beef, along with the water, to a skillet over medium heat. Mix well with a wooden spoon or spatula breaking up the meat as it cooks. Heat for 5 to 6 minutes, or until browned.
3. Microwave the refried beans in a microwave safe container on high for 90 seconds.
4. Place the flour tortillas on a plate and cover with plastic wrap. Heat the tortillas for 30 to 45 seconds in the microwave on high.

5. Build each burrito by first spreading about 1/4 cup of refried beans on the center of a heated flour tortilla. Spread one-eighth of the meat mixture over the beans, then pour about a tablespoon of the enchilada sauce over the meat.
6. Stir the sour cream, then spread about 1 1/2 tablespoons onto the burrito. Arrange your desired amount of lettuce, cheese, tomato, and onion onto the tortilla.
7. Fold the end of the tortilla closest to you over the filling ingredients. Fold either the left or right end over next. Then fold the top edge over the filling leaving one end of the burrito open and unfolded. Repeat with the remaining ingredients and serve immediately.

Makes 8 Burritos

*Taco Bell Enchirito

Ingredients

1 pound ground beef
1/4 teaspoon seasoning salt
1 teaspoon chili powder
1/2 tablespoon dried minced onion
1 can Taco Bell® refried beans
1/4 cup diced onion
1 can enchilada sauce
2 1/2 cups shredded Cheddar cheese
1 (2 oz.) can sliced black olives
1 package (10-12 inch) flour tortillas

1. Slowly brown the ground beef in a skillet using a wooden spoon or spatula to separate the beef into tiny pieces. Add the seasoning salt, chili powder and minced onion.
2. Using a potato masher, beat the refried beans until smooth. Heat beans as stated in the product instructions.
3. Spoon 3 tablespoons of beef into the center of each tortilla. Sprinkle on 1/2 teaspoon diced fresh onion. Add 1/3 cup refried beans.
4. Fold sides of each tortilla over the beans. Place the tortilla onto a plate. Spoon 3 tablespoons enchilada sauce over top of the tortilla.
5. Sprinkle 1/4 cup shredded cheese on the folded tortilla.
6. Microwave on high for 45 seconds or until cheese is melted. Top with 3 olive slices.

Serves 6

*Taco Bell Mexican Pizza

Ingredients

1/2 lb. ground beef
3 tablespoons Taco Bell® Taco Seasoning
2 tablespoons water
8 small flour tortillas
1 cup Taco Bell® refried beans - warmed
2/3 cup La Victoria enchilada sauce
1 cup shredded cheddar/Monterey Jack cheese blend
1/4 cup chopped tomatoes
1/4 cup chopped green onions

1. Using your hands, mix together beef, taco seasoning, and water.
2. Brown the beef mixture in a skillet over medium-high heat for 5-6 minutes, using a wooden spoon or spatula to break up the meat as it cooks; set aside.
3. Preheat oven to 375 degrees F.
4. In 375 degrees F oil, fry tortillas for 30-45 seconds per side or until golden brown. When frying each tortilla, be sure to pop any bubbles that form so that tortilla lays flat in oil. Drain tortillas on brown paper bags or paper towels.
5. When meat and tortillas are done, stack each pizza by first spreading about 1/3 cup refried beans on face of one tortilla. Next spread 1/4 to 1/3 cup of meat, then another tortilla. Coat your pizzas with two tablespoons of salsa on each, then split up the tomatoes and stack them on top. Next divide up the cheese, onions and olives, stacking in that order.
6. Place pizzas in oven until cheese has melted. Serve and enjoy.

Serves 4

*The Cheesecake Factory Cajun Jambalaya Pasta

This restaurant was started by Evelyn Overton in 1949 as a small scale bakery operated out of her family's basement in Detroit. Today they are a major chain and have much more on their menu than just cheesecake. However their cheesecake is still one of the best I've ever tasted.

Ingredients

4 oz. butter
2 teaspoons Cajun spice mix
1 pound boneless, skinless chicken breasts, cut into small pieces
1 pound fresh linguini pasta
1/2 cup clam juice
2 oz. green bell peppers, cut into thin strips
2 oz. red bell peppers, cut into thin strips
2 oz. yellow bell peppers, cut into thin strips
4 oz. red onions, cut into thin strips
1/2 pound fresh medium shrimp, peeled, de-veined, tails removed
1/2 cup diced tomatoes

1. Place the butter into a sauté pan on medium heat. Allow the butter to melt slightly. Add the seasoning into the pan and stir together with the melted butter. Add the chicken into the pan and continue to cook until the chicken is about half done.
2. While the chicken is cooking, carefully place the pasta into boiling water and cook until al dente (slightly chewy to the bite).
3. Pour the clam juice into the pan. Add the peppers and onions. Cook for another minute, making sure the vegetables are heated through and the chicken is almost done.

4. Add the shrimp into the pan. Toss the ingredients together and continue to cook until the shrimp are almost done.
5. Add the tomatoes into then pan. Continue to cook mixture until both the shrimp and chicken are thoroughly cooked through.
6. Place desired serving of pasta on a plate or in a bowl and add the jambalaya mixture.

Serves 4

*The Cheesecake Factory Chicken Fettuccini

Ingredients

1/2 lb fettuccini pasta
2 tablespoons olive oil
1 tablespoon garlic, chopped
6 medium mushrooms, sliced thin
1/4 red onions, julienned
1/4 cup white wine
1/4 cup chicken broth
1/2 grilled chicken breasts, julienned
1 tomato, peeled, seeded and diced
6 basil leaves, chopped
salt and pepper
2 tablespoons butter
parmesan cheese (to garnish)
green onions (to garnish)

1. Boil water, then add pasta. As pasta cooks, heat olive oil in a 12 inch sauté pan.
2. Add garlic to pan and saute for about 30 seconds.
3. Add red onions and mushrooms and saute for 2 minutes.
4. Add white wine and reduce by half, then add chicken broth and reduce by half.
5. Add tomatoes, basil and grilled chicken.
6. Saute 1 minute, then add butter to sauce.
7. Mix with cooked pasta.
8. Top with Parmesan Cheese and garnish with a few green onions and serve.

Serves 2-4

*The Cheesecake Factory Oreo Cheesecake

Ingredients

I (20 oz.) package Oreo cookies
I/3 cup unsalted butter, melted
3 (8 oz.) packages cream cheese (at room temp.)
3/4 cup sugar
4 eggs, at room temperature lightly beaten
I cup sour cream (at room temp.)
I teaspoon vanilla extract
whipped cream - to garnish (optional)
additional Oreo cookies, halved - to garnish (optional)

1. Finely crush 26-30 cookies and set aside.
2. Coarsely chop remaining cookies and set aside.
3. Mix together finely crushed cookie crumbs and melted butter.
4. Press cookie/butter mixture on the bottom and two inches up the sides of a 9-inch springform pan and set aside.
5. Beat cream cheese and sugar in bowl with electric mixer at medium speed until creamy.
6. Blend in lightly beaten eggs, one at a time, stirring by hand, to mix well after each addition.
7. Stir in sour cream and vanilla, until well blended.

8. Fold chopped cookies into the cheesecake batter.
9. Pour mixture into prepared crust.
10. Bake at 350°F for 55 to 60 minutes or until set.
11. Cool on wire rack at room temperature for about 15 minutes.
12. Run a thin blade knife around the inside of the pan between the pan and crust, being careful not to cut into the cake.
13. When cooled to room temp, refrigerate for at least 4 hours.
14. Remove side from pan; garnish with whipped cream, and a cookie half.

Serves 12-16

*The Cheesecake Factory Pumpkin Cheesecake

Ingredients

Crust
2 cups graham cracker crumbs
1 tablespoon of sugar
1 teaspoon cinnamon
5 tablespoons melted butter

Filling
1 pound cream cheese, room temperature
1 cup sour cream
1-1/4 cups sugar
1 teaspoon vanilla
3 tablespoons brown sugar
1 (15 oz) can pumpkin puree
2 teaspoons pumpkin pie spice
1/2 teaspoon cinnamon
4 eggs, lightly beaten

Crust:

1. Mix until crumbly, not pasty. Pat into 9" springform pan forming the crust along the bottom and up the sides. Set aside.

Filling:

1. Preheat oven to 350 degrees F.
2. In a mixer - beat cream cheese, sour cream, sugar and vanilla until smooth. Add pumpkin and spices and blend. Add eggs and blend again until mixed. Pour into pan over the crust.
3. Bake 40-45 minutes.
4. Turn oven off and leave the cheesecake in the oven for an additional 30 minutes.
5. Remove form oven. Refrigerate several hours until cheesecake cools and firms.
6. Garnish with whipped cream and nuts (optional).

Serves 10-12

*The Soup Nazi Crab Bisque

Remember the rules. Stay in line, quickly place your order and no small talk, or else "No soup for you!" The Soup Nazi was a character made famous on the popular sitcom "Seinfeld." The soup is said to be so good that customers are willing to follow the Soup Nazi's strict rules. The company - Soup Kitchen International located in New York City - received a lot of publicity from the show and is now offering franchising opportunities nationwide.

Ingredients

4 lbs. snow crab clusters (legs)
4 quarts water
1 small onion, chopped
1 1/2 stalks celery, chopped
2 cloves garlic, quartered
2 potatoes, peeled and chopped
1/4 cup fresh chopped Italian parsley
2 teaspoons mustard seed
1 tablespoon chopped pimento
1 16-oz. can refried beans
1/2 teaspoon coarse ground pepper
2 bay leaves
1/3 cup tomato sauce
1/4 cup heavy whipping cream (to thicken soup)
1/4 cup unsalted butter
1/4 teaspoon thyme
1/8 teaspoon basil
1/8 teaspoon marjoram (an herb)
2 tablespoons Old Bay Spice

1. Remove all the crab meat from the shells and set it aside.
2. Put half of the shells into a large pot with 4 quarts of water over high heat. Add onion 1 stalk of chopped celery, and garlic, then bring mixture to a boil. Continue to boil for 1 hour, stirring occasionally, then strain stock. Discard the shells, onion, celery and garlic, keeping only the stock.

3. Measure 3 quarts of the stock into a large sauce pan or cooking pot. Add water if there's not enough stock to measure 3 quarts.
4. Add potatoes, bring mixture to a boil, then add 1/2 of the crab and the remaining ingredients to the pot and bring it back to boiling. Reduce heat and simmer for 4 hours, uncovered until it reduces by about half and starts to thicken. Add the remaining crab and simmer for another hour until the soup is very thick.
5. Refrigerate overnight and reheat for best results.

Serves 4-6

*The Soup Nazi Cream of Sweet Potato Soup

Ingredients

4 (1 lb) sweet potatoes
4 cups chicken broth
4 cups water
1/3 cup butter
1/2 cup tomato sauce
3 tablespoons half and half
1 teaspoon salt
1/8 teaspoon pepper
2 tablespoons thyme
1 cup cashews (split in half)
1/4 cup diced canned pimento
1 jalapeno, diced
1/4 cup chopped Italian parsley
2 teaspoons chili powder
2 teaspoons basil
2 teaspoons oregano
1 clove garlic, minced
2 teaspoons cumin
1/4 teaspoon salt
dash cayenne pepper
sour cream (optional)
pinch chopped Italian parsley (optional)

1. Preheat oven to 375 degrees F. Bake the sweet potatoes for 45 minutes or until they are soft. Cool the potatoes before handling.
2. Peel away the skin, then put the sweet potatoes into a large bowl. Mash the sweet potatoes for 15-20 seconds (they don't have to be completely smooth).
3. Spoon the mashed sweet potato into a large saucepan over medium high heat, add the remaining ingredients and stir to combine.
4. Once the soup begins to boil, reduce the heat and simmer for 60 minutes - until soup has thickened a bit. Serve and enjoy.

Serves 6-8

*The Soup Nazi Indian Mulligatawny Soup

Ingredients

16 cups water
6 cups chicken stock
2 potatoes, peeled & sliced
2 carrots, peeled & sliced
2 stalks celery, with tops
1/2 eggplant, peeled & diced
1 medium onion, chopped
1 cup frozen corn
2/3 cup roasted red peppers, diced
1/2 cup tomato sauce
1/2 cup shelled pistachios
1/2 cup roasted cashews
1/2 cup chopped Italian parsley
1/4 cup lemon juice
3 tablespoons sugar
1/2 teaspoon curry powder
1/2 teaspoon pepper
1/4 teaspoon thyme
1 bay leaf
1 dash marjoram
1 dash nutmeg

1. Use a hand held mixer to puree all of the ingredients. It's ok if there are small chunks left.
2. Combine all mixture in a large pot over high heat.
3. Bring to a boil, then reduce heat and simmer, uncovered, for 5-6 hours or until soup has reduced by more than half and is thick. Stir several times throughout (and more frequently as it becomes thicker).
4. Refrigerate overnight and reheat for best results.

Serves 4-6

*The Soup Nazi Mexican Chicken Chili

Ingredients

4 chicken breast fillets
1 potato, peeled & chopped
1 small onion, diced
1 tablespoon olive oil
10 cups water
2 cups chicken stock
1/2 cup tomato sauce
1 cup frozen yellow corn
1/2 carrot, sliced
1 celery stalk, diced
1 cup canned diced tomatoes
1 15-oz. can red kidney beans, plus liquid

1. Pour olive oil into a large pot and sauté chicken in the olive oil over medium-high heat. Cook the chicken on both sides until done - about 8 minutes per side. Let chicken cool until it can be handled. Do not rinse the pot.
2. Break chicken up into small pieces by hand and while placing the pieces back into the pot.
3. Add the remaining ingredients to the pot and turn heat to high. Bring mixture to a boil, then reduce heat and simmer for 4-5 hours (the longer the better). Stir often. Chili will thicken and get browner when done.
4. Serve with a chopped Italian parsley and sour cream mixture on the side.

Serves 4-6

*Waffle House Waffles

Ingredients

1 1/2 cups all-purpose flour
1 teaspoon salt
1/2 teaspoon baking soda
1/2 cup granulated sugar
1/4 cup butter-flavored shortening
1 egg or equivalent of egg substitute
3/4 cup half and half cream
1/2 cup buttermilk
1/2 teaspoon vanilla extract

1. Combine flour, salt, and baking soda; set aside.
2. Cream together sugar, shortening, and egg with an electric mixer.
3. Gradually mix in half and half, buttermilk, and vanilla.
4. Add the dry flour mixture to the wet mixture while beating and mix until smooth.
5. Cover and refrigerate overnight.
6. Pour 1/2 cup of batter into a preheated, greased waffle iron and cook for 3-4 minutes, or until lightly browned. Repeat with remaining batter.

Serves 6

*Wendy's Chili

In 1969, at age 37, Dave Thomas quit his job at Arthur Treacher's to start the first Wendy's in Columbus, Ohio. While other hamburger chains at the time were using frozen beef and mass producing food, Dave Thomas developed an innovative way to make fresh, made to order fast food. His famous Chili has been on the Wendy's menu since it's inception.

Ingredients

2 lbs. ground beef
29 oz. can tomato sauce
1 1/2 cup water
29 oz. can pinto beans - undrained
29 oz can kidney beans - undrained
1 cup diced onion
1/2 cup diced green chili
1/2 cup diced celery
3 medium tomatoes, chopped
2 teaspoons ground cumin
3 tablespoons chili powder
1 1/2 teaspoons black pepper
2 teaspoons salt
dash garlic

RecipeSecrets.net tip:
If desired, serve with grated cheese, chopped green onion and sour cream on top. For the health conscious chili lovers you can substitute ground beef with ground turkey meat.

1. Cook ground beef in a skillet over medium-high heat until brown. Drain fat.
2. Break up beef into small crumbled pieces using a fork.
3. Stir beef and remaining ingredients into a large pot over low heat.
4. Simmer for about 2 hours, stirring occasionally.

Serves 10

*Wendy's Mandarin Chicken Salad

Ingredients

Sesame Dressing:
1/2 cup corn syrup
3 tablespoons white distilled vinegar
2 tablespoons pineapple juice
4 teaspoons granulated sugar
1 tablespoon light brown sugar
1 tablespoon rice wine vinegar
1 tablespoon soy sauce
1 teaspoon sesame oil
1/4 teaspoon ground mustard
1/4 teaspoon ground ginger
pinch salt
1/8 teaspoon paprika
dash garlic powder
dash pepper
1/2 cup vegetable oil
1/2 teaspoon sesame seeds

Mandarin Chicken Salad
4 chicken breast fillets
1 (10 oz.) package ready-to-serve salad or 4 cups torn iceberg lettuce
4 cups red leaf lettuce, chopped
1 1/3 cup canned mandarin orange wedges
1 cup rice noodles
1 cup roasted sliced almonds

1. Blend the first 14 sesame dressing ingredients (excluding vegetable oil and sesame seeds) in a blender on high. Gradually add in vegetable oil and sesame seeds and blend for a few seconds. Set dressing aside in refrigerator to chill.
2. Rub each chicken breast fillet with oil, then lightly season each piece with salt and pepper. Grill chicken over medium heat until done. Chill chicken breasts in refrigerator until cold.
3. Once chicken is cold, the next step is to build each salad. Place the iceberg lettuce in a salad bowl and add the red leaf lettuce on top.

4. Dice each chicken breast into small pieces and sprinkle the pieces over each salad.
5. Arrange about 1/3 cup of mandarin orange wedges on each salad. Next, sprinkle about 1/4 cup of rice noodles and 1/4 cup of almonds on top of each salad. Add sesame dressing and serve.

Serves 4

HELPFUL COOKING TIPS

1. Always chill juices or sodas before adding to beverage recipes.

2. Store ground coffee in the refrigerator or freezer to keep it fresh.

3. Seeds and nuts, both shelled and unshelled, keep best and longest when stored in the freezer. Unshelled nuts crack more easily when frozen. Nuts and seeds can be used directly from the freezer.

4. To prevent cheese from sticking to a grater, spray the grater with cooking spray before beginning.

5. Fresh lemon juice will remove onion scent from hands.

6. Instant potatoes are a good stew thickener.

7. Three large stalks of celery, chopped and added to about two cups of beans (navy, brown, pinto, etc.), will make them easier to digest.

8. When cooking vegetables that grow above ground, the rule of thumb is to boil them without a cover.

9. A scoop of sugar added to water when cooking greens helps vegetables retain their fresh color.

10. Never soak vegetables after slicing; they will lose much of their nutritional value.

11. To cut down on odors when cooking cabbage, cauliflower, etc..., add a little vinegar to the cooking water.

12. Perk up soggy lettuce by soaking it in a mixture of lemon juice and cold water.

13. Egg shells can be easily removed from hard-boiled eggs if they are quickly rinsed in cold water after they are boiled.

14. Keep bean sprouts and jicama fresh and crisp up to five days by submerging them in a container of water, then refrigerating them.

15. When trying to reduce your fat intake, buy the leanest cuts you can find. Fat will show up as an opaque white coating or can also run through the meat fibers, as marbling. Stay away from well-marbled cuts of meat.

16. Pound meat lightly with a mallet or rolling pin, pierce with a fork, sprinkle lightly with meat tenderizer, and add marinade. Refrigerate for about 20 minutes, and you'll have tender meat.

17. Marinating is easy if you use a plastic bag. The meat stays in the marinade and it's easy to turn and rearrange.

18. It's easier to thinly slice meat if it's partially frozen.

19. Tomatoes added to roasts will help to naturally tenderize them.

20. Cut meats across the grain; they will be easier to eat and have a better appearance.

21. When frying meat, sprinkle paprika over it to turn it golden brown.

22. Always thaw all meats in the refrigerator for maximum safety.

23. Refrigerate poultry promptly after purchasing. Keep it in the coldest section of your refrigerator for up to two days. Freeze poultry for longer storage. Never leave poultry at room temperature for more than two hours.

24. If you're microwaving skinned chicken, cover the baking dish with vented clear plastic wrap to keep the chicken moist.

25. Lemon juice rubbed on fish before cooking will enhance the flavor and help maintain a good color.

26. Scaling a fish is easier if vinegar is rubbed on the scales first.

27. Over-ripe bananas can be peeled and frozen in a plastic container until it's time to bake bread or cake.

28. When baking bread, a small dish of water in the oven will help keep the crust from getting too hard or brown.

29. Use shortening to grease pans, as margarine and oil absorb more readily into the dough or batter (especially bread).

30. To make self-rising flour, mix 4 cups flour, 2 teaspoons salt, and 2 tablespoons baking powder, and store in a tightly covered container.

31. Hot water kills yeast. One way to tell the correct temperature is to pour the water over your forearm. If you cannot feel either hot or cold, the temperature is just right.

32. When in doubt, always sift flour before measuring.

33. When baking in a glass pan, reduce the oven temperature by 25 degrees.

34. When baking bread, you get a finer texture if you use milk. Water makes a coarser bread.

35. To make bread crumbs, toast the heels of bread and chop in a blender or food processor.

36. Cracked eggs should not be used as they may contain bacteria.

37. The freshness of eggs can be tested by placing them in a large bowl of cold water; if they float, do not use them.

38. Dust a bread pan or work surface with flour by filling an empty glass salt shaker with flour.

39. To slice meat into thin strips for stir-fry dishes, partially freeze it so it will be easier to slice.

40. To keep cauliflower white while cooking, add a little milk to the water.

41. A roast with the bone in will cook faster than a boneless roast. The bone carries the heat to the inside more quickly.

42. For a juicier hamburger, add a little cold water to the beef before grilling.

43. To freeze meatballs, place them on a cookie sheet until frozen. Transfer to plastic bags and return to the freezer.

44. When boiling corn, add sugar to the water instead of salt. The salt will toughen the corn.

45. To ripen tomatoes, put them in a brown paper bag in a dark pantry.

46. To keep celery crisp, stand it upright in a pitcher of cold, salted water and refrigerate.

47. When cooking cabbage, place a small tin cup or can half full of vinegar on the stove near the cabbage. It will absorb the odor.

48. Potatoes soaked in salt water for 20 minutes before baking will bake more rapidly.

49. Let raw potatoes stand in cold water for at least a half-hour before frying in order to improve the crispness of French-fried potatoes. Dry potatoes completely before adding to oil.

50. A few drops of lemon juice in the water will whiten boiled potatoes.

51. Buy mushrooms before they "open." When stems and caps are attached firmly, they are fresh.

52. Do not use metal bowls when mixing salads. Use wood or glass.

53. Lettuce keeps better if you store it in the refrigerator without washing it. Keep the leaves dry. Wash the lettuce before using.

54. Never use soda to keep vegetables green. It destroys the Vitamin C.

55. If you over-salt your gravy, stir in some instant mashed potatoes to repair the damage. Add a little more liquid if necessary.

56. After stewing chicken, cool in broth before cutting to add more flavor.

COOKING TERMS

Au gratin: Topped with crumbs and/or cheese and browned in an oven or under a broiler.

Au jus: Served in its own juices.

Baste: To moisten foods during cooking with pan drippings or special sauce in order to add flavor and prevent drying.

Bisque: A thick cream soup.

Blanch: To immerse in rapidly boiling water and allow to cook slightly.

Cream: To soften a fat, like butter, by beating it at room temperature. Butter and sugar are often creamed together.

Crimp: To seal the edges of a two-crust pie either by pinching them at intervals with the fingers or a fork.

Crudites: An assortment of raw vegetables that is served as an hors d'oeuvre.

Degrease: To remove fat from the surface of stews and soups.

Dredge: To coat lightly with flour, cornmeal, breadcrumbs, etc.

Entree: The main course.

Fold: To incorporate a delicate substance into another substance without releasing air bubbles.

Glaze: To cover with a glossy coating, such as a melted and diluted jelly for fruit desserts.

Julienne: To cut vegetables, fruits, or cheeses into match-shaped pieces.

Marinate: To allow food to stand in a liquid in order to tenderize or to add flavor.

Mince: To chop food into very small pieces.

Parboil: To boil until partially cooked; to blanch.

Pare: To remove the outer skin of a fruit or vegetable.

Poach: To cook gently in hot liquid kept just below the boiling point.

Saute: To cook food in a small amount of butter/oil.

Simmer: To cook in liquid just below the boiling point.

Steep: To let food stand in hot liquid in order to extract or enhance the flavor.

Toss: To combine ingredients with a repeated lifting motion.

Whip: To beat rapidly in order to incorporate air and produce expansion.

HERBS & SPICES

Basil: Sweet, warm flavor with an aromatic odor. Use whole or ground. Good with lamb, fish, roasts, stews, ground beef, vegetables, and dressings.

Bay Leaves: Pungent flavor. Use whole leaf but remove before serving. Good in vegetable dishes, seafood, stews and pickles.

Caraway: Spicy taste and aromatic smell. Use in cakes, breads, soups, cheese and sauerkraut.

Chives: Sweet, mild flavor like that of onion. Excellent in salads, fish, soups and potatoes.

Cilantro: Use fresh. Great in salads, salsa, fish, chicken, rice, beans and other Mexican dishes.

Curry Powder: Spices are combines to proper proportions to give a distinct flavor to meat, poultry, fish and vegetables.

Dill: Both seeds and leaves are flavorful. Leaves may be used as a garnish or cooked with fish, soup, dressings, potatoes, and beans. Leaves or the whole plant may be used to flavor pickles.

Fennel: Sweet, hot flavor. Both seeds and leaves are used. Use in small quantities in pies and baked goods. Leaves can be boiled with fish.

Ginger: A pungent root, this aromatic spice is sold fresh, dried, or ground. Use in pickles, preserves, cakes, cookies, and meat dishes.

Marjoram: May be used both dried or green. Use to flavor fish, poultry, omelets, lamb, stew, stuffing and tomato juice.

Mint: Aromatic with a cool flavor. Excellent in beverages, fish, lamb, cheese, soup, peas, carrots and fruit desserts.

Oregano: Strong and aromatic. Use whole or ground in tomato juice, fish, eggs, pizza, chili, poultry, vegetables.

Paprika: A bright red pepper, this spice is used in meat, vegetables and soups or as a garnish for potatoes, salads or eggs.

Parsley: Best when used fresh, but can be used dried. Try in fish, omelets, soup, meat and mixed greens.

Rosemary: Very aromatic. Can be used fresh or dried. Season fish, stuffing, beef, lamb, poultry, onions, and potatoes.

Saffron: Orange-yellow in color, this spice flavors or colors foods. Use in soup, chicken, rice and breads.

Sage: Use fresh or dried. The flowers are sometimes used in salads. May be used in fish, beef, poultry, cheese spreads and breads.

Tarragon: Leaves have a pungent, hot taste. Use to flavor sauces, salads, fish, poultry, tomatoes, eggs, green beans and dressings.

Thyme: Sprinkle leaves on fish or poultry before broiling or baking. Add a few sprigs directly on coals shortly before meat is finished grilling.

ARE YOUR HERBS & SPICES FRESH?

Ingredient Shelf Life:

- Ground Spices 2-3 years
- Whole Spices 3-4 years
- Seasoning Blends 1-2 years
- Herbs 1-3 years
- Extracts 4 years, except pure vanilla, which lasts forever

Still not sure, then use these guidelines:

Check to see that the color of your spices and herbs is vibrant. If the color has faded, chances are so has the flavor.

Rub or crush the spice or herb in your hand. If the aroma is weak and flavor is not apparent, it's time to replace it.

Store herbs and spices in a tightly capped container, and keep away from heat, moisture, and direct sunlight. Replace bottle lids tightly immediately after use.

To minimize moisture and caking, use a dry measuring spoon and avoid sprinkling directly into a steaming pot.

- Check the freshness date on the container.

GUIDELINES FOR BUYING FRESH VEGETABLES

Artichokes: Look for compact, tightly closed heads with green, clean-looking leaves. Avoid those with leaves that are brown or separated.

Asparagus: Stalks should be tender and firm; tips should be close and compact. Choose the stalks with very little white; they are more tender. Use asparagus soon after purchasing because it toughens rapidly.

Beans: Those with small seeds inside the pods are best. Avoid beans with dry-looking pods.

Broccoli, Brussels Sprouts, Cauliflower: Flower clusters on broccoli and cauliflower should be tight and close together. Brussels sprouts should be firm and compact. Smudgy, dirty spots may indicate pests or disease.

Cabbage and Head Lettuce: Choose heads that are heavy for their size. Avoid cabbage with worm holes and lettuce with discoloration or soft rot.

Cucumbers: Choose long, slender cucumbers for best quality. Avoid yellow ones.

Mushrooms: Caps should be closed around the stems. Avoid black or brown gills.

Peas and Lima Beans: Select pods that are well-filled but not bulging. Avoid dried, spotted, yellow, or flabby pods.

GUIDELINES FOR BUYING FRESH FRUITS

Bananas: Skin should be free of bruises and black or brown spots. Purchase green and allow them to ripen at home at room temperature.

Berries: Select plump, solid berries with good color. Avoid stained containers which indicate wet or leaky berries. Berries without clinging caps, such as blackberries and raspberries, may be unripe. Strawberries without caps may be overripe.

Melons: In cantaloupes, thick, close netting on the rind indicates best quality. Cantaloupes are ripe when the stem scar is smooth and the space between the netting is yellow or yellow-green. They are best when fully ripe with fruity odor.

Honeydews are ripe when rind has creamy to yellowish color and velvety texture. Immature honeydews are whitish-green.

Ripe watermelons have some yellow color on one side. If melons are white or pale green on one side, they are not ripe.

Oranges, Grapefruit and Lemons: Choose those heavy for their size. Smoother, thinner skins usually indicate more juice. Most skin markings do not affect quality. Oranges with a slight greenish tinge may be just as ripe as fully colored ones. Light or greenish-yellow lemons are more tart than deep yellow ones. Avoid citrus fruits showing withered, sunken or soft areas.

MEASUREMENTS

a pinch	1/8 teaspoon or less
3 teaspoons	1 tablespoon
4 tablespoons	1/4 cup
8 tablespoons	1/2 cup
12 tablespoons	3/4 cup
16 tablespoons	1 cup
2 cups	1 pint
4 cups	1 quart
4 quarts	1 gallon
8 quarts	1 peck
4 pecks	1 bushel
16 ounces	1 pound
32 ounces	1 quart
1 ounce liquid	2 tablespoons
8 ounces liquid	1 cup

Use standard measuring cups and spoons.
All measurements are level.

RECIPES BY CATEGORY

Appetizers

Breakfast

Desserts

Entrees

Salads

Side Dishes

Soups

Miscellaneous

TRADEMARKS

- Applebee's is a registered trademark of Applebee's International, Inc.
- Auntie Anne's is a registered trademark of Auntie Anne's, Inc.
- Benihana is a registered trademark of Benihana, Inc.
- Bennigan's is a registered trademark of Metromedia Restaurant Group.
- Boston Market is a registered trademark of Boston Market Corporation which is a wholly owned subsidiary of McDonald's Corporation.
- Burger King and Burger King Whopper are registered trademarks of Burger King Corporation.
- California Pizza Kitchen is a registered trademark of California Pizza Kitchen, Inc.
- Chi-Chi's is a registered trademark of Chi-Chi's, Inc. and Prandium, Inc.
- Chili's is a registered trademark of Brinker International.
- Cinnabon is a registered trademark of AFC Enterprises, Inc.
- Dairy Queen is a registered trademark of International Dairy Queen, Inc. and Berkshire Hathaway Inc.
- El Pollo Loco is a registered trademark of El Pollo Loco, Inc.
- Hard Rock Café is a registered trademark of Hard Rock America, Inc.
- Hooters is a registered trademark of Hooters of America.
- Houston's is a registered trademark of Bandera Restaurants.
- IHOP and International House of Pancakes are registered trademarks of International House of Pancakes, Inc.
- Joe's Crab Shack is a registered trademark of Landry's Seafood Restaurants, Inc.
- Junior's Cheesecake is a registered trademark of Juniors Restaurant & Cheesecakes Inc.
- KFC, Taco Bell, and Long John Silver's are registered trademarks of Yum! Brands, Inc.
- Macaroni Grill is a registered trademark of Brinker International.
- McDonald's and the Big Mac are trademarks of McDonald's Corporation.

- Olive Garden is a registered trademark of Darden Restaurants, Inc.
- Outback Steakhouse is a registered trademark of Outback Steakhouse, Inc.
- Panda Express is a registered trademark of Panda Restaurant Group, Inc.
- P.F. Chang is a registered trademark of P.F. Chang's China Bistro, Inc.
- Planet Hollywood is a registered is a registered trademark of Planet Hollywood, Inc.
- Popeyes is a registered trademark of AFC Enterprises, Inc.
- Red Lobster is a registered trademark of Darden Restaurants, Inc.
- Ruby Tuesday is a registered trademark of Morrison Restaurants, Inc.
- Sara Lee is a registered trademark of Sara Lee Corporation.
- Shoney's is a registered trademark of Shoney's, Inc.
- Sizzler is a registered trademark of Sizzler International, Inc.
- Starbucks is a registered trademark of Starbucks Corporation.
- The Cheesecake Factory is a registered trademark of The Cheesecake Factory, Inc
- The Soup Nazi is a registered trademark of Soup Kitchen International.
- T.G.I. Friday's is a registered trademark of T.G.I. Friday's, Inc.
- Waffle House is a registered trademark of Waffle House, Inc.
- Wendy's is a registered trademark of Wendy's International, Inc.

To find a restaurant near you, please visit:

Applebee's	http://www.applebees.com
Auntie Anne's	http://www.auntieannes.com
Benihana	http://www.benihana.com
Bennigan's	http://www.bennigans.com
Boston Market	http://www.bostonmarket.com
Burger King	http://www.burgerking.com
California Pizza Kitchen	http://www.cpk.com
Chi-Chi's	http://www.chichissalsa.com
Chili's	http://www.chilis.com
Cinnabon	http://www.cinnabon.com
Dairy Queen	http://www.dairyqueen.com
El Pollo Loco	http://www.elpolloloco.com
Hard Rock Cafe	http://www.hardrockcafe.com
Hooters	http://www.hooters.com
Houston's	http://www.hillstone.com
IHOP	http://www.ihop.com
Joe's Crab Shack	http://www.joescrabshack.com
KFC	http://www.kfc.com
Macaroni Grill	http://www.macaronigrill.com
McDonald's	http://www.mcdonalds.com
Olive Garden	http://www.olivegarden.com
Panda Express	http://www.pandaexpress.com
P.F. Chang's	http://www.pfchangs.com
Planet Hollywood	http://www.planethollywood.com
Popeyes	http://www.popeyes.com
Red Lobster	http://www.redlobster.com
Ruby Tuesday	http://www.rubytuesday.com
Sara Lee	http://www.saralee.com
Shoney's	http://www.shoneys.com
Sizzler	http://www.sizzler.com
Starbucks	http://www.starbucks.com
Taco Bell	http://www.tacobell.com
The Cheesecake Factory	http://www.thecheesecakefactory.com
The Soup Nazi	http://www.soupkitchenintl.com
T.G.I. Friday's	http://www.fridays.com
Waffle House	http://www.wafflehouse.com
Wendy's	http://www.wendys.com

- RECIPE FAVORITES -